# Kitchen of Love

*recipes to feed your soul*

Compiled under the guidance and inspiration of

**SWAMI BV NARAYANA**

Join us on www.kitchenoflove.com

The **Kitchen of Love** is a collaborative book project that was compiled under the guidance and loving inspiration of our Gurudeva, Srila Bhaktivedanta Narayana Gosvami Maharaja, by Yasodanandan das (text), Bhanumati dasi (recipes) and Raghava Pandit das (design). There were many contributors to the completion of this book in the form of art, design, editing, advice, layout, proofreading, research, recipes, typing, and typesetting, including: Sriman Premananda Prabhu, Sripada Padmanabha Maharaja, Sripada Vaikhanas Maharaja, Sripada Bhagavat Maharaja, Sripada Nemi Maharaja, Srimati Syamarani didi, Sripada Tridandi Maharaja, Srimati Vaijayantimala dasi, Anupama dasi, Gokuldas das, Yasomatinandana das, Krishna-Priya dasi, Sarojini dasi, Nandasuta das, Tamal-Krishna ji, Kilimba dasi, Radhanath das, Shilpakarini dasi, HariPriya dasi & Anuradha dasi (NZ), Jayanti dasi & Mamata dasi, Shashikala dasi & Ananga Mohini dasi (NL), Madhavananda das & Snigdha dasi, Bela dasi & Dhruva das (NZ), Premananda das (Italy), Andrius Valatka, Ananga Mohini dasi (UK), Sundar Gopal das & Mohini dasi, Sudevi dasi & Kishori-mohan das, Vishvambara das, Kamala dasi (UK), Ashta Sakhi dasi, Shyam das (UK), Radhakanta das (USA), Gopinath ji, The Punja family, Damayanti dasi (AU), Chrissie Hynde (Krishnamayi), Vasanta das, Radha-Madhava das & Nagari dasi (NL), Nimai Caitanya das, Karla, Eva and Teresa ji, Vijay-Krishna, Sarasvati & the Kirtaniyas. Many thanks!



**ISBN: 978-90-817679-2-7**

Kitchen of Love may be purchased in bulk at special discounts for sales promotion, gifts, fund-raising, or educational purposes. For details, contact info@bhaktimedia.org

# Contents

“Love has nothing to take, yet every-thing to give...”

– Swami BV Narayana

# Preface

This work has been inspired by my Guru, Tridandiswami Sri Srimad Bhaktivedanta Narayana Maharaja. He is a master practitioner of bhakti-yoga, or "devotional love". He lived a life of service from 1921-2010. He did not leave India until 1996 and then, during his last fourteen years, travelled the world thirty-one times and wrote over one hundred books. Throughout the book, I refer to him as "Gurudeva". A guru is a person who takes his follower from the "gu", that is the "darkness" to the "ru" which is the "light".

The **"Kitchen of Love"** has been developed by collaborating with many wonderful people across the world. Recipes have been sent in from around the world. I have interviewed at least thirty people. I am so grateful for this collaboration and for the patience shown by so many as I asked endless questions. In the "Kitchen of Love" many cooks have "enhanced the broth" and not spoiled it!

Yasodanandan das

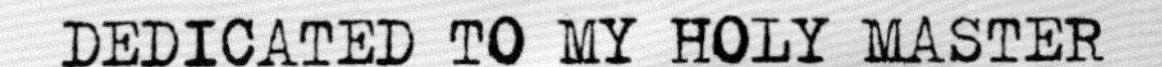

# DEDICATED TO MY HOLY MASTER

who dedicated his life to spreading the sublime philosophy of Bhakti-Yoga, the devotional love of God, throughout the world.

## *Srila Gurudeva*

Sri Srimad Bhaktivedanta
Narayana Gosvami Maharaja

# The Principle of Love

"The principle of love, the current of love does not consider any obstacles on the way. It crosses all rules and regulations, and there is no principle of religion that controls it. It has its own law and tradition. The heart and theme of love is that one who loves will always be very careful about the desires of his lover. He will not impose his desires on his lover, but will instead minutely observe what his worshipable deity wants..."

— Swami BV Narayana

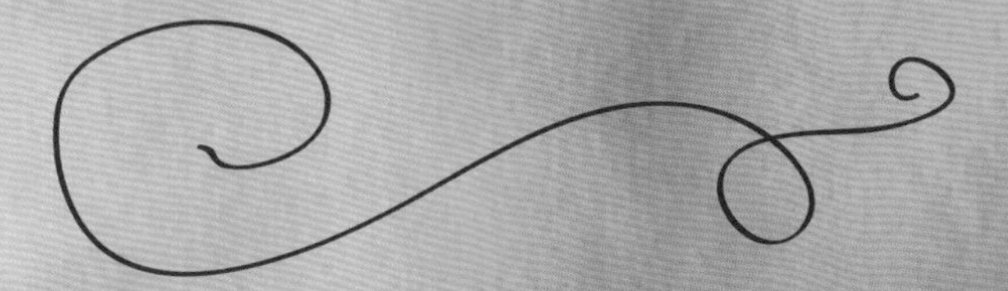

"My natural response was to share this experience with someone else. ... This is the spirit of the book."

# Introduction

Welcome to the "Kitchen of Love". This cookbook works on two levels. First, it includes delicious vegetarian recipes. Every recipe has been designed for maximum taste and is accompanied by photographs to provide inspiration. Second, the book is interspersed with quotes and stories of my spiritual experiences. This is why it is called "Kitchen of Love". In India, the preparation of food plays an intrinsic role in the expression and development of the individual's spirituality. I have found this very attractive which is why I am sharing it with you.

The spiritual path I have taken is known as bhakti-yoga, or the path of "devotional love". I am aware that, in today's world, "God" and "religion" are sensitive words. Fundamentalism, terrorism, a history of wars and horrendous repression as well as a lack of respect of women's rights have all made us, rightly, very wary.

I do not seek to convince anyone that this concept of God is right or wrong, better or worse, or that He even exists. I just happened to stumble, "Forest Gump" style, across an ancient spiritual method I wasn't even looking for. And, over many years it has provided me with experiences of love, depth and richness for which I am profoundly grateful. I remember when I was seven years old how enthusiastic I was to learn something new. The natural response was to share this experience with someone else. This is the quality of raw human enthusiasm. This is the spirit of the book.

On the one hand, I do not wish to impose any ideas onto anyone. I want to share with the mood of the innocent child who has learned something new and desires to reach out and connect with people. A child like this has no agenda and no plan. The child wants to play, share and have fun with other children. Therefore, this book is presented as a spiritual experience and not a religious presentation. On the other hand, as my spiritual journey involved such an intimate introduction to God, it would strip the book of meaning if I did not refer to Him. For the reader's convenience, therefore, a short explanation of the treasure that is ancient India's conception of God is provided below.

## God, The Vedas & Love

One of the obstacles to learning a language at school is that the experience is disconnected from the cultural source. When I learned French at school I never went beyond formulating my words in English, translating in my head and then speaking French. It was only when I lived in France, shopped in their markets and dined with my local hosts daily that the language made sense and I started to think and feel in French.

This disconnect can also be felt when trying to impart my spiritual experiences of "God" in India. Although my first trip to India in 1996 was only an eleven-day immersion, it was so profound that my whole conception and cultural context for God shifted just as my thinking in French did many years previously.

The Indian conception of God rests upon a vast body of ancient knowledge, both written and orally passed down the generations. These are known as the Vedas and the ancient Indian civilisation is known as the "Vedic" civilisation. Today's scholars estimate the dawn of this era to be between 3,500 and 5,000 years ago. Practitioners consider its glory has been extant since the beginning of time. Their deepest understanding of God, passed down, generation after generation, is extraordinary.

In this world, we often talk about "falling in love". Entire movie industries have been built upon this emotion. When we fall in love, each person wants to do anything for the other. True love involves always wanting to sacrifice for the other. My pleasure is derived from pleasing my beloved. After a period of time, this "in love" feeling can wane if we revert to selfish behaviour. Perhaps the highest love on Earth is that of a mother to her child. It is the ultimate in unconditional love.

These examples of material love depend upon there being a lover and a beloved. When I arrived in India, what struck me was that their culture recognised a deeply personal relationship with God. I felt that I could be His beloved, in a purely pristine way, and that I could get to know Him in an intimate way. I was born a Jew and was educated at Christian schools. Although I never subscribed to the image, God was always portrayed to me in vague terms as an old gentleman with a beard in the sky. I never understood Whom I was supposed to be worshipping.

In India, the old culture gives the aspiring lover of God a very colourful, fun, playful and varied description of God, His friends and associates and all His pastimes. I would ride on a rickshaw early in the morning and come across another rickshaw with ten gorgeous little Indian children on their way to school, all neat in their school uniforms. Arms aloft I would cry out "Krishna!" or "Jai Krishna!" or "Jai Radhe!". "Jai" means "glory to" and "Krishna" is the masculine aspect of the Supreme Personality of Godhead. "Radha" is the feminine. Even though I am a stranger and a foreign one, ten ecstatic little voices would respond to me in unison. Throughout the book, therefore, I refer to God as either "God", "Krishna", "Radha", "Radha-Krishna" or "the Supreme Personality of Godhead."

During the day, through one happenstance encounter or another, I was served food first offered to Krishna, with love and devotion and with no desire to convert me to anything. This is the cultural context for my experience of God, or Krishna, in India, and it was most often expressed through eating with the locals. It is this journey, connected to an ancient civilisation 5,000 years ago and passed down through great sages down the millenia, that I am grateful to be able to share with you now. I hope that you experience this access not only through these words, but also the colours, smells and taste of the recipes included herein.

"There is only one language in the world, and that is the language of love."

— Swami BV Narayana

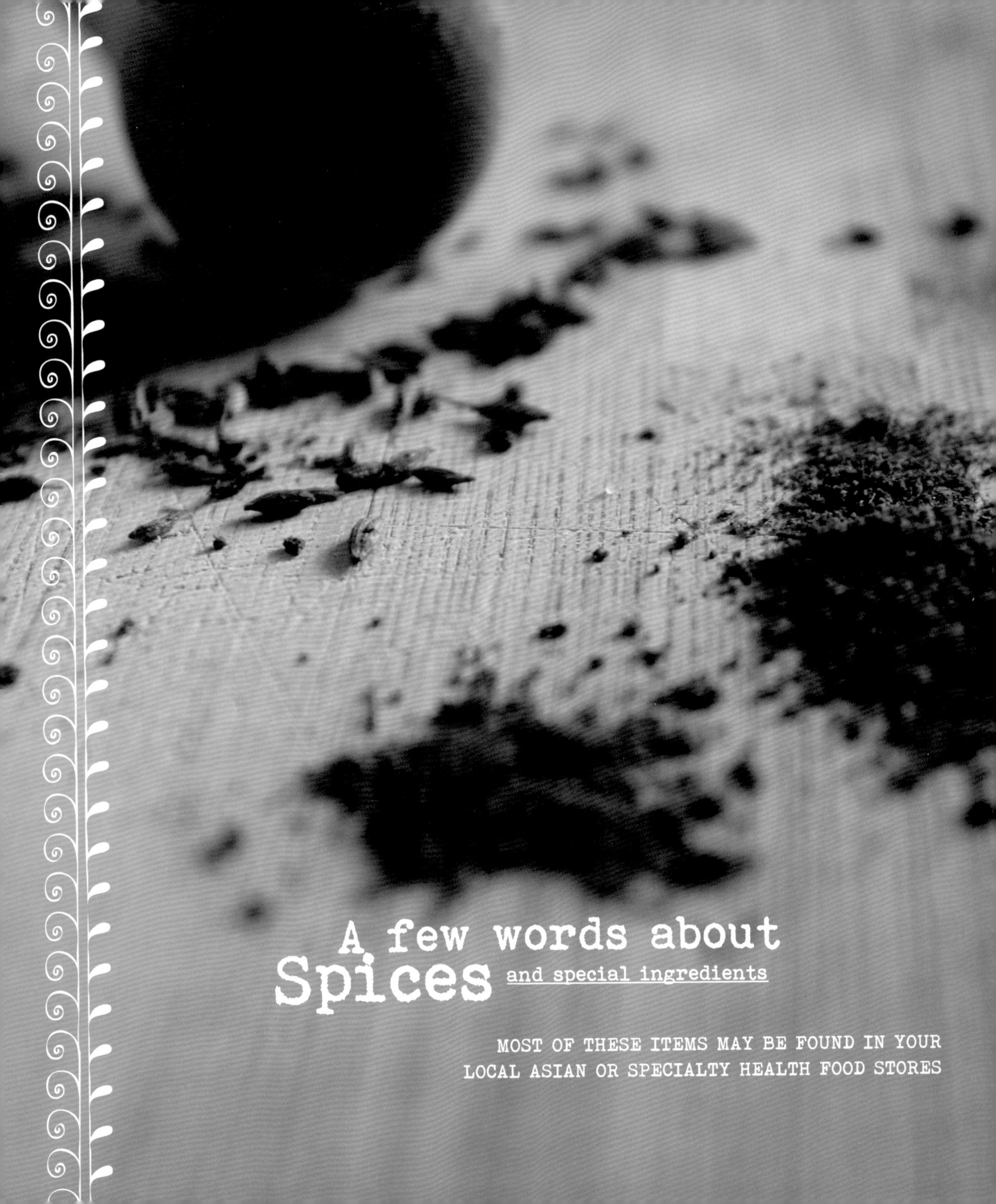

# A few words about Spices and special ingredients

MOST OF THESE ITEMS MAY BE FOUND IN YOUR LOCAL ASIAN OR SPECIALTY HEALTH FOOD STORES

**Agave nectar**
From the agave plant, this natural sweetener is 1.4 to 1.6 times sweeter than sugar. Often substituted for sugar recipes, also for the vegan alternative to honey in cooking. Because it dissolves quickly, it can be used as a sweetener for cold beverages.

**Atta flour**
Used to make Asian flatbreads such as chapati, roti, naan and poori. Most atta is milled from the semi-hard wheat varieties, also known as durum wheat, that comprise 90% of the Indian wheat crop. Doughs made out of atta flour are strong and can be rolled out very thin.

**Asafoetida (Hing)**
Dried gum from the root of the ferula plant. It is pungent and often used in cooking to replace onions and garlic. Medicinally, used as a digestive aid. Available as pure gum (very potent) or as compound hing (the yellow powder). We use the compound and brand 'Vandevi'. If using the pure form, reduce the quantities by 3/4.

**Besan flour**
Also known as gram flour is made from hulled chickpeas, or chana dal. It has a slightly nutty flavor and earthy aroma. The high-protein content makes it ideal for the large vegetarian population in India. Used as a thickener in curries, to make fritters (pakoras) or savory pancakes called pudla.

**Curry Leaves**
Used throughout India to flavour dals and curries. Prevents diseases and obesity. The dried leaves are not as strong as the fresh leaves.

**Ghee**
Clarified butter is the pure butter fat with out the milk solids. It has a high smoke point, meaning that it can withstand high temperatures without becoming harmful to health, and has a unique sweet flavor.

**Hemp flour**
Produced by pressing the oil from the hemp seed, and milling the residue. Hemp seed (and flour) contain a large dietary supplement of omega-3. It gives a spongy nutty texture and flavour.

**Himalayan Salt**
Rock salt, white and/ or pinkish-red appearance. Analysis of Himalayan salt has shown that it contains ten different minerals and it is this nutritional benefit that has made it the choice of health-conscious cooks.

**Kaffir Lime Leaf**
Used in South East Asian cuisine, this leaf from a tree of the citrus family has an aromatic, astringent flavor, similar to the lime itself.

**Kolonji seeds**
The nigella seeds have a pungent bitter taste and smell, often referred to as black cumin. It is used in 'Panch Puran', a mixture of five spices originating from Bengal, India.

**Mung Dal**
Protein-rich dried and split mung beans are used in Indian cuisine mainly as dal, a soup-like dish. Two kinds include the whole mung beans or quicker-cooking yellow split mung dal.

**Mustard Oil**

Has a high smoke point and is therefore suitable for cooking at higher temperatures. It is made from grinding mustard seeds and therefore has a rather pungent flavour.

**Paneer**

This fresh curd cheese is the Indian equivalent to tofu. It is made by adding a curdling agent (lemon juice or citric acid) to boiling milk, so that the solids and whey separate. To make, heat 2 liters of milk, add 3 tbsp lemon juice at boiling point, drain and press using a very fine colander or cheese- cloth. Makes 1 1/2 cups paneer. Great in various dishes.

**Quinoa**

Originally from South America, not strictly a grain as it does not belong to the grass family, but can be treated as one in cooking. It is an excellent source of protein, magnesium, phosphorous and iron, and is also gluten- free.

**Saffron**

Golden yellow-orange threads (collected from the saffron crocus) used as a delicate spice. Its aroma is often described as reminiscent of honey with grassy or hay-like notes, while its taste is hay-like and sweet. It has a long medicinal history as part of traditional healing and has antioxidant properties.

**Tahini**

A paste made of finely ground sesame seeds, used in Middle Eastern and Eastern Mediterranean cuisine. It is a good source of calcium in particular, therefore has found favour amongst vegans as a substitute for dairy products in sauces and spreads.

**Tapioca**

A starch extracted from cassava. Tapioca is commonly used as a thickener agent for puddings, sweets, soups and other delicacies. It is available in different forms such as pearls, flour and flakes. The pearls were used in this book.

**Tempeh**

Firm in texture and earthy flavors, a whole soybean product originating from Indonesia. Tempeh's fermentation process and its retention of the whole bean give it a high content of protein, dietary fiber and vitamins.

**Turmeric (Haldi)**

Yellow powder dried from a pungent-bitter, slight astringent root and one of the most important Ayurvedic spices. It helps digest proteins, is antibacterial, anti-tumor, anti-viral, anti-inflammatory, anti-Alzheimer, anti-cancer and an antioxidant.

# How to use Measurements

As this is a collaborative book project, different cooks have shared their recipes. Most of them cook with their 'heart and feeling' rather than using 'exact' measurements.

The recipes in this book were prepared using the American and British cooking measurements. You will see the American standard converted into metric weights and volume.

All conversions are approximate and most have been rounded up or down to the nearest whole number.

Small volumes (3 tablespoons and under) such as salt, herbs, spices, baking powder, etc. were converted into milliliters rather than grams.

The cup converts to 240 milliliters for liquids.
The cup converts to ounces or grams for non-liquids.
The tablespoon converts to 15 ml.
The teaspoon converts to 5 ml.

**The abbreviations in the recipes are as follows:**

- Tablespoon: tbsp
- Teaspoon: tsp
- Pounds: lbs
- Ounces: oz
- Kilogram: kg
- Grams: gr
- Liters: l
- Milliliters: ml
- Fahrenheit: °F
- Celsius: °C

Learn more on www.kitchenoflove.com

# Love

"Every time we eat we can become ever evolving, heart softening conscious beings of ripening love."

It is not just milk that sustains us when we are babies and we cry for our mothers. It is love. When we strip life back, when we look beyond the world of status, money, others' perceptions and the infinite variety of distractions available to us, I always come back to love and affection. It is love that makes the difference. It is love that makes it worth being alive.

However, the world does not always seem constructed to get this best side of me – the feeling, devoted, conscious person. Do you often feel short of time? Sometimes, I notice it is 11 o'clock at night and I cannot remember what I did that day because it all moved with such a pace, in a kind of blur of actions and obligations. Where was "I" in all of that? Do you feel that your experiences, your "transactions" with other people, can sometimes be shallow and lacking in intimacy or emotional nourishment?

I went to a detox centre last year. It was in Turkey. Every day I walked down to the beach past a shop displaying a bounty of succulent, in-season, fruits. However, as I was "detoxing", I was not eating. So, every day I would approach the shop owner. He was old and each day of his life seemed etched onto his face like an old tree trunk. He usually sat on a wooden chair with a cigarette in one hand and a stick in the other. We spoke not of word of each other's language. But somehow we laughed, and counted down the end of my fast when I could buy his wonderful produce. He gesticulated that we should arm wrestle each other. I felt nourished. I had time. Each moment had value.

This book is about my experiences bringing a deep sense of presence into the day's moments, cherishing life and each other. It is about how we can pour love into food and food into love. It is how every time we eat we can become ever-evolving, heart-softening conscious beings of ripening tenderness.

However, this journey goes deeper. It goes to the very source of all amour—the amour of the Supreme Personality of Godhead. When we feel truly cherished by God, without the subtle or gross coercion of society, then we can walk around complete, full, without the need to be constantly distracted. This book shares experiences as to how a few simple changes to the way we take our meals can impact this process in a profoundly spiritually positive way.

For most of my life I have wanted to understand some fundamental questions. How do we truly relate to each other? How do we relate to animals? How do we relate to God? How do we relate to Nature and what is the significance of all these things we have like houses and cars?

When travelling to India for the first time in 1996, I discovered how practitioners of bhakti-yoga (devotional love) find a deep connection with the Supreme Lord by preparing their food in a sacred way, full of gratitude and offering it to Him first. While this made the preparation and eating of food a profound and more poignant experience, it did not mean it had to take any longer. I experienced ten thousand people being served such special food known as "prasadam" very efficiently. And I noticed how this experience deepened a sense of unity amongst thousands of people, many of whom did not know each other. It enriched individuals' relationships with themselves and with the Lord of all worlds. In this book, I would like to share this principle of devotion with you. If you choose to practise this sacred food preparation and it works for you, it can add to your daily experiences. It brings a sense of increased connection with that Supreme Personality and with yourself in a very intimate and relaxed manner. I liked this because this sacred way of preparing food gave me a way of communicating with Him without the need to join any religious organisation.

# Mercy

"As experienced practitioners of Bhakti Yoga, they were eager to serve us prasadam. "Prasadam" literally means "mercy" in the ancient Indian language, sanskrit."

When I first went to India I met a wonderful gentleman who is in charge of one of the main Radha-Krishna temples of Vrindavana. Vrindavana is a very holy place in India. He and his wife were always having my wife, Ananga Mohini, and I for lunch or dinner or, for that matter, we could stay the night and then have breakfast whenever we wanted. It was only later that we realised they moved out and were giving us their bedroom! As experienced practitioners of bhakti-yoga, they were eager to serve us prasadam. Prasadam literally means "mercy" in the ancient Indian language, Sanskrit.

In my slightly awkward English way, I felt it a bit cumbersome. Being invited to one or two dinners without inviting them back was tolerable. But what happens when you reach fifteen? However, they did not see this as an economic or a social transaction. It was not even traditional hospitality. Their motivation came from a deeper and more sublime place. They were serving Radha-Krishna by serving us. This gentleman would serve us prasadam and would not eat until we were satisfied. It was quite unsettling to begin with. On the one hand he was always happy when I took seconds and thirds. The more helpings I had, the longer he would have to wait for his meal. I soon learned that this latter concern of mine was a misconception. My satisfaction was his satisfaction because he knew that by pleasing me was actually pleasing Krishna. I was honouring the prasadam by partaking of it. And he was honouring the prasadam by serving it. In effect we were both enjoined in a dance of devotion with Krishna. In the practice of bhakti-yoga, he knew God as Krishna. Krishna is not an old man with a beard but, in His original form, a most beautiful, eternal youth of fourteen, who is all-attractive. The way this gentleman practised, Krishna felt close and real, and not far away and remote.

When I started my spiritual life, I did what most people do. Whatever imbalances prevailed in my everyday life I applied in my spiritual life, for better and worse. Blind to my own nature, I immediately started to strive. I wanted to get somewhere. I thought that I could run up the ladder to Radha-Krishna at full pace and get there first!

I did not realise that spiritual life is a very different experience and requires a different mood. There is a wonderful saying by Albert Einstein: "We cannot solve our problems with the same thinking we used when we created them." I was well on my way to trying. I was striving, forcing and pushing more than accepting, receiving and giving. However, something about prasadam (mercy) struck me. An old friend of mine had repeated a key teaching taught from ancient India's epic, Bhagavad-Gita. He kept on reminding me that "you are not the doer".

Think about it. Did you conceive yourself? Did you give birth to your own body? Do you control your organs? Can you control when you die? Can you control the weather, the sun or the moon? It dawned on me how little we really control and yet how hard this is to accept.

Then I realised that, in many ways, our spiritual evolution is not in our control either. I was taught the concept of "causeless mercy". I was told that Krishna loves me unconditionally. It is not about making Krishna love me. It is about realising and feeling that He already does. It is not that we get touched by the affection of the Supreme Personality of Godhead because we are in any way materially better. This mercy, the abundance of compassion and

पत्रं पुष्पं फलं तोयं यो मे भक्त्या प्रयच्छति ।
तदहं भक्त्युपहृतमश्नामि प्रयतात्मनः ॥ २६ ॥

In the Bhagavad-gita (9.26) Shri Krishna says:

*patraṁ puṣpaṁ phalaṁ toyaṁ*
*yo me bhaktyā prayacchati*
*tad ahaṁ bhakty-upahṛtam*
*aśnāmi prayatātmanaḥ*

*If one offers Me with love and devotion a leaf, a flower, a fruit or water, I will accept it.*

love, is there for everyone to receive if they want it.

Prasadam is one of the core components of the mercy available to you and me as set out in the philosophy of bhakti-yoga. Krishna, through His causeless mercy, is not asking us to be super-heroes of spiritual self-denial. He is making it easy for us. He is saying to me that I have my five senses. And of those five senses, the tongue is the strongest, the most rapacious. It likes to eat and talk. However, engage the tongue with mercy, prasadam, and, by serving the supreme Lord Sri Krishna, my consciousness can evolve into an unfathomably intimate relationship with God.

I realized that Krishna wants to relish me – my soul – as I am in essence, and that a spiritual path is not about changing myself out of any sense of material inadequacy. Instead, it is about recognizing how merciful and attractive Krishna is. Then, over a period of time, as I absorb this mercy, the parts of me that

*Turn to page 114 to learn about the process of sanctifying your food and turning an ordinary meal into a sacred offering of love and devotion.*

he Divine Couple
Radha-Krishna

are devoid of devotion will fall away naturally and my soul will shine through with intensity. As time goes on, this temporary conditioning evaporates and my heart will soften as I become more aware of my true self, the soul.

This is why vegetarianism is such an important part of bhakti-yoga. Within every living body there is a living entity, a soul. This is the real and eternal part of who we are. Our bodies and minds are temporary. They are like clothes that are put on and taken off. Who we really are, the soul, remains covered by this temporary body. Souls are particles of consciousness capable of the highest yearning for Krishna. We all have the capability to evolve towards a higher and higher state. However, we cannot commit violence upon one another and, at the same time, develop a heart soft enough to be a receptacle for the mercy that is so abundant and available. Remember how your heart feels when you have a bitter argument with a loved one. Then imagine how it feels if there is violence between you and a cherished one. Now think of the violence that you are ingesting into your body when you eat other animals.

In the United States, six billion animals are slaughtered every year for our pleasure. The number of chickens eaten in a single day today equates to the number eaten in an entire year in 1930. We all have a brotherly and sisterly connection to each other and all animals because Krishna loves us all, and we all have the full potential to feel that affection and offer our service accordingly.

But how can we soften our hearts enough to be present to the prevailing mercy if we anaesthetise ourselves by participating in this daily violence and suffering?.

In my case, the change to vegetarianism was swift. I was nineteen and I had managed to get a job as a goat herder in south-west France before I went to university. I can't say I was a great goat herder. The two dogs did most of the work! However, when the farm owner fed me a meal consisting of goat meat and vegetables, the connection between the meat on my dinner plate and the group greeting I received from the goats the next day became too irreconcilable. From then on it was vegetarianism for me.

It helps to offer your food to Krishna. He does not accept any food containing animal flesh—no red meat, no white meat, no fish and no eggs. Offer what you can—rice, lentils, tofu, fruit, salad, vegetables, yoghurts, milk products and cakes. As we offer vegetarian food to Krishna, we start to extricate ourselves from this cycle of violence. By offering our food to Krishna, we are transforming it into mercy, which we directly ingest and benefit from. We can digest as much of this mercy as our hearts can be soft and open enough to accept. We can then journey back to Godhead, back to our true intimate relationship with our beloved Krishna.

*And of all yogis,*
*the one who always abides in Me*
*with great faith, thinks of Me within himself,*
*and renders transcendental loving service to Me — he*
*is the most intimately united with Me in yoga and is the*
*highest of them all. That is My opinion.*

SRI KRISHNA IN THE GITA 6.47

To sanctify =
to satisfy

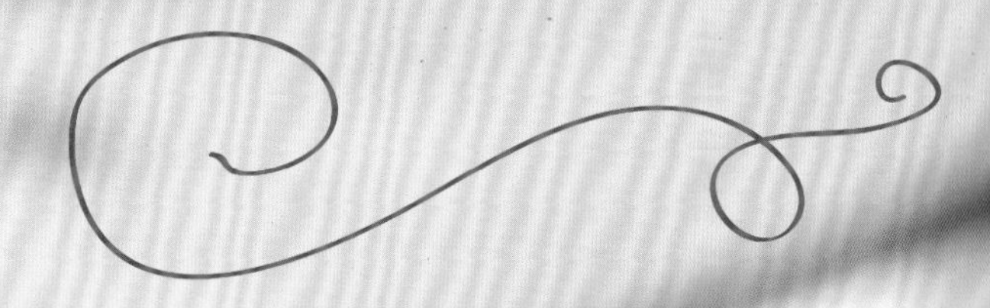

## All you need is

- 1 cup (240 gr) split yellow mung beans
- 6 cups water (1440 ml)
- 1 cup potato* (180 gr) cubed into 1 inch (2.5 cm) pieces
- 1 cup cauliflower* (200 gr) cut in small florettes
- 1 cup zucchini (courgette)* (180 gr) cubed into 1 inch (2.5 cm) pieces
- 1 cup tomatoes (160 gr) chopped in small pieces
- 1 1/2 tbsp (20 ml) ghee or oil
- 1 tsp (5 ml) cumin seeds
- 1/2 tsp (2.5 ml) dark mustard seeds
- 1 tbsp (15 ml) dried curry leaves
- 1 tbsp freshly grated ginger
- 1 green chili, seeded and finely chopped
- 1 tsp (5 ml) asafoetida
- 1 tsp (5 ml) turmeric
- 1 tbsp salt (15 ml or to taste)
- Fresh coriander (cilantro) leaves to garnish
- Lime slices to garnish
- Plain yoghurt to garnish

* Potato, cauliflower and zucchini (courgette) are optional or can be substituted for other veggies.

by Anuradha dasi & Haripriya dasi

# Dal - Indian Yellow Split Pea Soup

**Serves 4 - preparation & cooking time 40-45 minutes**

## THE WAY

1. Rinse beans until water runs clear.
2. Bring beans, water, turmeric to a boil then bring heat to medium-low, keeping a soft rolling boil, until beans begin to breakdown and become soft (10-15 minutes).
3. Stir occasionally, watch for and remove the froth from the top of the boiling water.
4. Once soft, add potato and cauliflower and raise heat until boils again, cook for a few minutes, bring heat to medium-low, and add zucchini (corgette).
5. Put ghee or oil in small saucepan on medium-high heat until hot. Add mustard and 1/2 tsp of the cumin seeds until they start to sizzle and pop then add curry leaves stirring until fragrant. Turn down heat slightly, add ginger and chili, let sizzle again and add asafoetida, stirring for several seconds.
6. Stir this spice mixture into the dal along with salt, tomatoes and simmer.
7. Dry roast 1/2 tsp cumin seeds in a hot frying pan until a darker roasted color and becomes fragrant. Remove from heat and grind seeds with a mortar and pestle. Sprinkle fresh ground cumin over dal (without stirring) and cover with a lid.
8. Prepare garnishes, then stir the dal and serve.

# Tomato Chutney

**Serves 4-6 - Preparation & cooking 20 min.**

- 1 1/2 lbs (700 gr) ripened tomatoes
- 3 tbsp (15 ml) ghee or oil
- 1/2 tsp (2.5 ml) asafoetida
- 1/2 tsp (2.5 ml) mustard seed
- 1/2 tsp (2.5 ml) ground cumin
- 1/2 green chili (or 1 red dried chili) seeded and finely chopped
- 1 small cinnamon stick (optional)
- 2 cloves (optional)
- 2 tsp (10 ml) salt (or to taste)
- 3 tbsp (35 gr) brown sugar

1. Boil tomatoes whole until skin wrinkles and cracks (5-10 min). Drain tomatoes, put aside. Once cooled, peel off the skins and mash. (Keep some of the stock for thinning later on if needed.)
2. Heat the ghee or oil on medium-high heat in deep pan, add mustard seeds until they sizzle and pop then add the asafoetida, cumin, chili and the tomato.
3. Add the cinnamon and the cloves.
4. Boil until it starts to thicken, approximately 10 minutes.
5. Season with salt, add sugar, stir and turn off the stove.
6. Before serving remove cinnamon stick and cloves to finish.

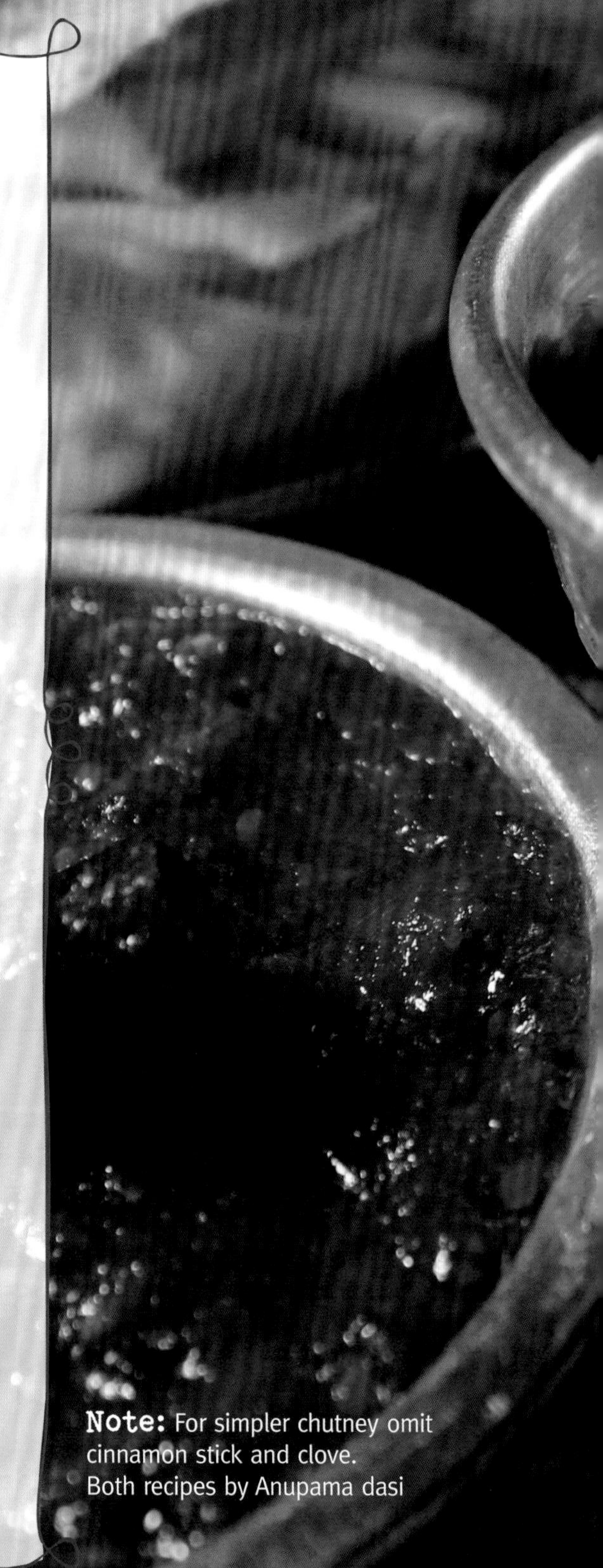

**Note:** For simpler chutney omit cinnamon stick and clove.
Both recipes by Anupama dasi

# Ghobi (Cauliflower) Pakoras

Serves 4 - Preparation & cooking time 30 minutes

## All you need is

- 1.2 lbs (500 gr) cauliflower
- 3/4 cup (75 gr) besan (gram/chickpea) flour
- 1/4 cup (40 gr) plain flour
- 3 tbsp (45 gr) rice flour
- 1 tbsp (15 ml) coriander powder
- 1 tsp (5 ml) baking powder
- 1/2 tsp (2.5 ml) turmeric
- 1/2 tsp (2.5 ml) asafoetida
- 3/4 – 1 cup (175 – 240 ml) cold water
- 1 1/2 tsp (7.5 ml) salt
- Ghee or oil for deep-frying

1. Combine all dry ingredients well, add half of the water and mix thoroughly with a whisk, removing all the lumps.
2. Gradually add the remaining water (not necessarily the rest) to form a smooth batter that will sufficiently coat vegetables while frying.
3. Let the batter sit while cutting up the cauliflower (cut into approx. 30 bite size pieces).
4. Heat the ghee or oil on medium-high. Cook until golden brown, and then drain on a paper towel.
5. Serve with tomato chutney.

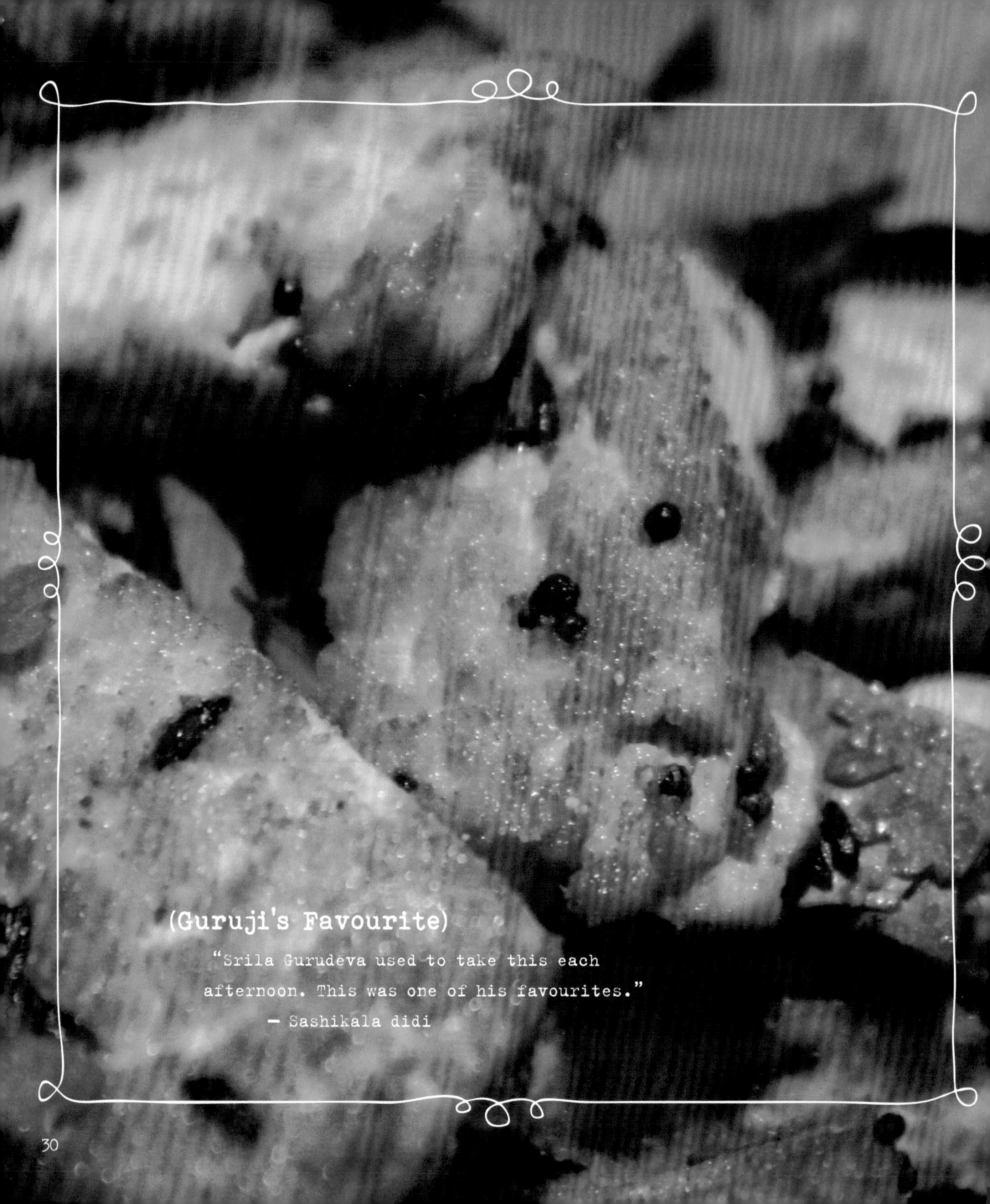

(Guruji's Favourite)

"Srila Gurudeva used to take this each afternoon. This was one of his favourites."
— Sashikala didi

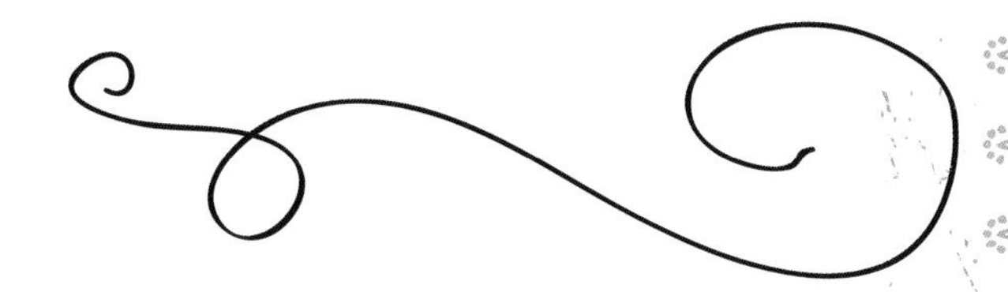

# Pan-fried Tofu

**Serves 4 - preparation and cooking time 15 minutes**

## Method

1. Mix the tofu with the turmeric and salt in a bowl until tofu is evenly covered with these two spices.
2. Put the olive oil in non-stick pan on medium heat.
3. When the oil is heated put the cumin, mustard and kolonji seeds in the pan and stir-fry seeds until they sizzle and pop for 1 minute.
4. Add the tofu to the pan and fry until all sides are golden brown.
5. Add asafoetida and stir-fry for 30 seconds.
6. Put the fried tofu into a bowl, add finely chopped coriander leaves and lightly mix.

Serve with rice, roasted eggplant, cooked spinach and fried kerala.

## All you need is

- 1.4 lbs (650 gr) tofu cut into thin rectangular pieces 1 1/4 x 3/4 x 1/4 inches (3 cm x 2 cm x 1/2 cm)
- 2 tsp (10 ml) cumin seeds
- 1 tsp (5 ml) asafoetida
- 3 tsp (15 ml) turmeric
- 1 tsp (5 ml) black mustard seeds
- 2 tsp (10 ml) kolonji seeds (black)
- 2 tsp (10 ml) salt
- 3 tbsp (45 ml) olive oil

# Pan Roasted Eggplant (Guruji's Favourite)

Serves 4 as a side dish - preparation & cooking time 30-40 minutes

### All you need is

- 2 medium eggplants
- 1 tsp (5 ml) mustard oil
- 1 green chili seeded and finely chopped
- 1 tbsp (15 ml) olive oil
- 1/2 tsp (2.5 ml) dark brown mustard seeds
- 1/2 tsp (2.5 ml) coriander powder
- 1 tsp (5 ml) grated ginger
- 1 tsp (5 ml) salt
- Fresh coriander leaves finely chopped
- Olive oil to glaze eggplants

"I used to cook this every day in the afternoon time for Srila Gurudeva„

Recipe by Shashikala dasi

**Note:** heavy bottomed pans are best used for frying because they heat the oil to a higher heat and are faster due to having a larger area to heat. They also, store more heat, which makes browning and cooking more even.

### The way

1. Wash and dry the eggplants, then glaze the skin well with olive oil.
2. Put eggplants in a heavy bottom pan on medium heat and cover with a lid.
3. Cook on each side for 3 to 5 minutes. Repeat until all sides are roasted and crispy and the eggplants are soft inside. You will feel the softness when you try picking them up to turn over with tongs.
4. Take eggplants out of pan, cool for 5-10 minutes. Peel and mash them.
5. Put olive oil in a shallow frying pan on medium heat. When oil is heated, add mustard seeds, stir-fry until they start to sizzle and pop. Turn down the heat to low and add ginger, coriander powder, green chili and stir in pan.
6. Add the mashed eggplants in the pan and mix with the spices, add salt.
7. Turn off the heat and add mustard oil and fresh chopped coriander and lightly mix. This is ready to be offered.

Serve with rice, Guruji's favourite tofu and cooked spinach or fried kerala.

Offered by Bhanumati dasi, inspired by different cooks & their unique styles.

# Saucy Eggplant, Tomato +Paneer Subji

**Serves 4 - preparation and cooking time 40 minutes**

## All you need is...

- 1 large eggplant cut into 1/2 inch (1.5 cm) pieces
- 2 cups (12 oz or 350 gr) pre-made paneer into 1/2 inch (1.5 cm) cubes
- Ghee or oil for deep-frying paneer
- A deep pan of warm salted water to put fried paneer in to soak
- 1.5 lbs (600 gr) tomatoes, cut and blended into a fresh chunky puree
- Ghee or oil for pan-frying eggplant
- 1/2 tsp (2.5 ml) asafoetida to cook with eggplant
- 2 tbsp ghee or oil for cooking spices
- 1/2 tsp (2.5 ml) black mustard seeds
- 1 tsp (5 ml) cumin seeds
- 1 tbsp (15 ml) dried curry leaves
- 1 tbsp (15 ml) freshly grated ginger
- 1 tsp (5 ml) fresh green chili seeded finely chopped
- 1/2 tsp (2.5 ml) asafoetida to cook with spices
- 1/2 tsp (5 ml) turmeric
- 1 tsp (5 ml) ground cumin
- 1 tsp (5 ml) ground coriander
- 1 tsp (5 ml) garam masala
- 1 tsp (5 ml) sugar
- 1 tbsp (15 ml) creme fraiche (optional)
- 1 1/2 tsp (7 ml) salt (or to taste)

## The way

1. Cut eggplant, salt and place in-between paper towel sheets to let the water extract for 10 minutes, then pat until dry.

2. Heat ghee or oil in pan to deep-fry premade paneer until slightly browned. Put in warm salted water until ready to put in mixture last.

3. Cut tomatoes and put in blender to make a chunky puree.

4. Heat ghee or oil to medium heat in large flat pan, sprinkle oil with 1/2 tsp asafoetida and add eggplant. Pan-fry until browned, slightly crispy outside and tender inside (add more oil if needed while cooking) and put aside.

5. Heat 2 tbsp ghee or oil, in large wok or deep pot over medium heat. Add mustard and cumin seeds until they start to sizzle and pop. Turn heat down slightly, add ginger and chili, let sizzle and then add curry leaves and cook until fragrant. Add asafoetida stirring for a several seconds, add turmeric and stir for a few more. Add ground cumin, coriander, and tomato puree and cut tomatoes then cook for several minutes on medium-low heat.

6. Mix in sugar, garam masala, creme fraiche, salt, drained paneer (take out of water) and eggplant. Serve with rice and papadams.

**Tip:** you can buy pre-made paneer (Indian Cheese) or you can make your own. See the section on a few words about spices for more on paneer.

**Note:** Subji means 'vegetable dish', either wet or dry.

# Green Bean & Potato Subji

Serves 4 - preparation and cooking time 25 minutes

## All you need is

- 1.2 lbs (500 gr) potatoes cubed into 1 inch (2.5 cm) pieces
- 1/2 lb (250 gr) French beans, trim bottom and cut in half
- 1 1/2 tbsp (22.50 ml) ghee or oil
- 1/2 tsp (2.5 ml) cumin seeds
- 1/2 tsp (2.5 ml) mustard seeds
- 1/2 tsp (2.5 ml) asoefoetida
- 1/2 tsp (2.5 ml) ground cumin
- 1/2 tsp (2.5 ml) curry powder
- 1/2 tsp (2.5 ml) freshly grated ginger
- 1 cup (240 ml) water (you may need more)
- 2 tomatoes cut in half and then quartered
- 1 1/2 tsp (7.5 ml) salt (or to taste)
- Coriander leaves for garnish

## The way

1. Heat ghee or oil, in wide and heavy bottom pot over medium heat. Add mustard and cumin seeds until they start to sizzle and pop. Turn heat down slightly, add ginger and chili, let sizzle, add asafoetida stirring for a several seconds.

2. Put heat to medium, add potatoes and stir with spices for 1 minute.

3. Add water, cover pot with lid and cook at same heat for 1 minute. Then put heat to medium-low and cook for several minutes. Add beans and cook until potatoes are soft (you may need more hot water to finish cooking veggies).

4. Mix in ground cumin, curry powder, and cut tomatoes then cook for a few more minutes. Garnish with coriander leaves.

Recipe by Anuradha dasi
& Haripriya dasi

# Pooris
## (deep fried puffed breads)

**Serves 6 - preparation time 15-20 minutes - cooking time 30 minutes**

### All you need is

- 2 cups (480 gr) wholemeal atta flour* (chapati flour)
- 1/4 tsp (1.25 ml) salt
- 6 tbsp (90 ml) sunflower oil
- 3/4 - 1 cup lukewarm water (or as needed)
- Ghee or oil for deep-frying

### The way

1. Mix the atta, salt and oil together until it resembles a coarse-like consistency.
2. Add the water sparingly, slowly pouring to bind the dough together while kneading.
3. The consistency should be pliable dough.
4. Divide the dough into small-size balls and put aside.
5. Preheat the ghee or oil over low/medium heat.
6. Roll out the balls, with a rolling pin, individually into small disk-like shapes, carefully ensuring that the disks are even all over (not too thick or too thin).
7. Carefully slip the poori into the hot ghee/oil and wait for it to raise and puff all over. Wait until the poori is golden-brown and then turn over and repeat the process. Once both sides are evenly golden-brown, remove from the ghee/oil and set aside into a paper towel lined tray.

* You can find atta flour at Indian or Asian stores

Puris are most commonly served at breakfast. They're also served at special or ceremonial functions as part of ceremonial rituals along with other vegetarian food offered in prayer as 'prasadam'. The name puri derives from the Sanskrit word purika, from pura "filled".

Serve with eggplant, paneer subji, dal and healthy green chutney.

RECIPE BY MAMATA DASI & JAYANTI DASI

# Kitchari
## - a feast for yogis, kings & sadhus alike

Serves 4-6 - preparation and cooking time 40 minutes

### All you need is

- 1 cup (240 gr) split yellow mung beans
- 1 cup (240 gr) basmati rice
- 7 cups (1680 ml) water (you may add more later for desired thickness)
- 1 cup sweet potato (orange)* (180 gr) cubed into 1 inch (2.5 cm) pieces
- 1 cup cauliflower* (200 gr) cut in small florettes
- 1 cup zucchini (courgette)* (180 gr) cubed into 1 inch (2.5 cm) pieces
- 1 cup tomatoes (160 gr) chopped in small pieces
- 2 tbsp (20 ml) ghee or oil
- 1 1/2 tsp (7.5 ml) turmeric
- 1 tsp (5 ml) cumin seeds
- 1/2 tsp (2.5 ml) dark mustard seeds
- 1 green chili, seeded and finely chopped
- 1 tbsp freshly grated ginger
- 1 tsp (5 ml) asafoetida
- 1 tbsp coriander powder
- 1 tbsp salt (15 ml or to taste)
- Fresh coriander (cilantro) leaves to garnish
- Lime slices to garnish
- Plain yoghurt to garnish

*Potato, cauliflower and zucchini (courgette) are optional or can be substituted for other veggies such as bell peppers, pumpkin or string beans.

## The way

1. Rinse beans and rice until water runs clear.

2. Bring beans, rice, water and turmeric to a boil then bring heat to medium-low, keeping a soft rolling boil, until beans begin to breakdown and become soft (10-15 minutes).

3. Stir occasionally, watch for and remove the froth from the top of the boiling water.

4. Once soft, add potato and cauliflower and raise heat until boils again, cook for a few minutes, bring heat to medium-low, and add zucchini (courgette). Check if you want to add more water. Stir the bottom so it doesn't stick.

5. Put ghee or oil in small saucepan on medium-high heat until hot. Add mustard and cumin seeds until they start to sizzle and pop. Turn down heat down slightly, add ginger and chili, let sizzle again and add asafoetida and coriander powder stirring for several seconds.

6. Stir this spice mixture into the kitchari along with salt, tomatoes and simmer.

7. Prepare garnishes, then stir the dal and serve.

**Note:** The ancient practice of fasting on kitchari, or a "kitchari cleanse", utilizes the traditional mix of rice and mung beans. In Ayurveda, the ancient wisdom of India dating back 5,000 years, this mix of rice and mung beans is considered extremely easy to digest and is said to purify the digestion and cleanse the body of toxins.

Offered by Raghava ji

ree Rādhā

CHANT

**Serves 4 - preparation time 5-10 minutes**

## All you need is

- 1 cup (240 gr) ripe mango pieces
- 1 cup plain (240 gr) yoghurt
- 1 cup (240 ml) water
- 1/2 cup ice cubes
- 1 tsp (5 ml) rose water
- 3-4 tbsp (36-48 gr) caster sugar

## The way

1. Put all ingredients into a blender for 30-60 seconds; add more of any ingredient depending on desired consistency and taste.

by HariPriya dasi

The Divine Couple
Shri Shri Radha & Krishna

# God & the Goddess

What better way to explore the possibilities of that devotion than to traverse over the realm of awe-of-God and sojourn to the place of forget-He-is-God?

I was born Jewish and attended a Christian school. I now deeply appreciate the mysticism and teachings of both religions. However, when I was growing up, neither pathways, as they were taught to me, captured my heart. I yearned for something experiential, something that touched me, something I could not deny as real.

I adored my Grandpa. But, every Saturday, I conspired with my Grandmother to pretend to be asleep so I would not have to go to synagogue. Then, once the door had shut, it was breakfast in bed time with Grandmother. It was so much fun! Although I didn't please Grandpa by not going to synagogue, we used to spend many happy hours after he returned from synagogue as he stroked my head and related to me his early memories. The stories came from his childhood between 1905 and 1909 of Cossacks burning his Russian village and his fear as he lay hidden under straw in a cart. I was captivated and wanted him to go on forever. I was experiencing something in my heart. I was gripped.

I wandered throughout my childhood having lonely one-to-one chats with God, never sure who I was speaking with but determined not to get drawn into any religious process that did not further the experiential dimension of my relationship with Him. Without a sense of intimate relationship, I felt, faith was a misapplied resource.

When I started travelling to India in 1996, I was amazed how villagers I met were living and breathing their relationships with Krishna every day. Ordinary people were connected through this family. Spiritual experiences were not compartmentalised. What deeply struck me, and still does, is their concept of loving Krishna by forgetting that He is God. To begin with this sounded strange, and then I got it and it nourished my soul.

I never took to the idea of worshipping God based on fear. I was just not attracted. Perhaps I was too naughty! I just felt that if He only wanted me to fear Him, then I just could not relate. I couldn't pretend. And then I learned in the Vaisnava tradition what God in the spiritual world looks like, what are His qualities, and who are His friends and family. This way we get to know, intimately, His character and ways. Most strikingly, it was explained, God (or Krishna) had created a potency which makes Him forget He is the Lord of all. At the same time, all His friends and family remained oblivious to this fact.

This made perfect sense to me. How can you intimately cherish Krishna if you are always overwhelmed that He is God almighty? You can love almighty God; but, if both you and Krishna forget He was God, then how much sweeter would that amour be for Krishna? It would be so sweet.

In the spiritual world, Krishna loves to play with his friends. They wander off into the forest together and laugh and play and eat together. Some of the most beautiful stories relate to Krishna's mother, Yasoda. She churns the butter each day. She wants to make buttermilk for her darling son and she cries in happiness as she thinks of Him while churning. She becomes anxious when she hears stories about her mischievous son stealing butter from her neighbours. In reality, however, all her friends are secretly hoping that Lord Krishna will steal their butter because their hearts overflow for Him and they adore cooking for Him!

Imagine a President of a country or a Prime Minister. When they get home after a day of being fawned upon at several formal events, they look forward to their kids charming them and not treating them with any awe. Krishna (the Supreme Personality of Godhead) desires to taste our love for Him. What better way to explore the possibilities of that devotion than to traverse over the realm of awe-of-God and sojourn to the place of forget-He-is-God?

Most wonderful are the stories of Radha-rani, also known as Sri Radha. Not only are the spiritual experiences about love and not fear, but the Supreme Godhead is acknowledged as both male and female. Indeed, my Guru, Tri-dandiswami Sri Srimad Bhaktivedanta Narayan Maharaj, who had taken me under his wing since 1996, always praised Radha's love as being higher than Krishna's.

Yasoda knew that Krishna relished Radha's food. She would send one of Krishna's cousins to request that Radha come to cook at home for Krishna. Krishna would know which preparations had been made by Radha and He would know she was watching Him taste it, hidden from view. In the morning, He would sometimes pretend not to like the dish, teasing Radha and intensifying Her mood of love towards Him. The ecstatic love between Radha and Krishna is often indirect in this way. Krishna pretends that He does not a particular sweet or dish. This compels Radha to taste it and, thereby, taste His remnants. She is tasting the love that Krishna has experienced from the love that Radha put in the food – which became prasadam after it was offered to Krishna – in the first place when She made it. This intensifies the mood of affection between The Divine Couple.

In the spiritual world, it is explained how the exchange of love and tenderness between Krishna and His beloved friends and family is often through food. If we can spiritualise our experience here on Earth, then we can gradually experience this most intimate part of Krishna's love directly.

We offer our food by prayer to Gurudeva who does not eat it but, in turn, offers it to Radha and Krishna. Radha offers the food to Krishna. He relishes it as He can taste Her ardour for Him in it. She then eats the prasadam and relishes His pleasure, which is imbued in the prasadam. She shares the prasadam with Her friends, and then She gives the prasadam back to Gurudeva. He relishes Their love. He then bestows the mercy, the prasadam, to me and whomever I am serving.

How poetic, intimate and beautiful that by this simple process, I can receive the mercy of the Divine Couple. This way my heart can be pierced a million times by their arrows of compassion and Their boundless, wondrous affection can flow through me and I become totally satisfied.

# Prema = Divine Love & Affection

If one is fully initiated but does not have love and affection for Krishna, then ones offering of foodstuffs by mantra and 16 kinds of paraphernalia, will not be accepted by Krishna.

On the other hand, if you have prema, Krishna will have so much hunger for taking whatever you offer and thinks, "When My devotee offers anything to Me, I will take it. I will accept it, because My devotee possesses prema." Whatever such a pure devotee brings to Krishna – although he has not yet offered it – Krishna will run after him to take it...

– Swami BV Narayana

# The Soul

"By taking blessed foodstuffs...,
our souls will shine brighter."

One day my wife, Ananga, was sitting in front of Srila Gurudeva, introducing her brother, Andrew. As usual around Gurudeva, the atmosphere was other-worldly, timeless and full of bliss. Gurudeva looked at Andrew and enquired, "What is your name?"

He replied: "Andrew".

Gurudeva then asked: "So, Andrew, what happens when you leave your body?" Andrew responded that his soul goes to heaven.

"So, are you looking after your body nicely?" Gurudeva enquired.

Andrew said: "Yes".

"And what are you doing for your soul?" he asked. A long silence followed as Andrew realised that he spent a lot of time looking after his body and material needs, and yet neglected his soul. It was a simple question. It made us all think.

Everything material is temporary. It will ultimately be destroyed. It is real but has only temporary value. It has no eternal value. If you think of most things you own, have acquired or have accomplished for the purpose purely of enjoyment, then you will recall how their value can be fleeting. It may be a house, a car or a piece of jewellery. It may a comfortable top or a great pair of jeans, but none of it compares to the deepest love you have felt for your mother or family, a sibling, a friend or a romantic partner. Then, imagine how this love compares to the intensity with which Radha-Krishna love you.

I was chatting with a friend from California recently. He runs a prasadam restaurant with his wife. They prepare everything from the very best organic produce. However, they do not explicitly make a big noise about the food being prasadam. The offering process is done quietly, without any of the customers knowing. He told me that every day customers would come up

**The customer suddenly says, "Do you pray over the food? Is that the difference?" Then my friend explains...**

to him and the conversation would go something like this. The customer would say: "That food was amazing. What do you guys put into it?" And my friend would answer: "Well, it's all vegan and organic and local." The customer would fire back: "No, no, there's something else, there is some special ingredient in there!" There would be an exchange of smiles and a pause until the customer would suddenly say: "Do you pray over the food? Is that the difference?" Then my friend would explain what he does.

I cherish this story. It shows me that there is an eternal part of each person that recognises things that have eternal value. The world is very simple from the perspective of the soul. There is you and I, there is God, and there are inanimate things. Our true identity is that we are soul. The soul is effortlessly in love with God. However, having been embodied in so many species of life since the beginning of time, we have forgotten Him. We have become fixated on the external, temporary world. Our five senses—taste, touch, smell, sight and sound—confuse us and we forget this natural state.

My wife, Ananga was reading to me a really interesting article about the concept of "chronos" and "kairos". Chronos is the time that you and I have to deal with every day. It is chronological time; being on time for meetings, being on time for a dinner or being on time when picking up your kid from school. Kairos is a moment of time when something special happens. In a modern version of Christian theology this developed into an appointed time when God acts. There are moments every day when you can stop and look at your list of things to do and say: "The world will not crumble if I take a few minutes to taste life more deeply and lay aside the world of constant motion." Preparing prasadam instead of just eating something expediently is a wonderful way to access this special time, and to place God very centrally into our life in a personal and intimate way.

By taking prasadam, the soul, who can only be satisfied by serving Krishna, by receiving value from the eternal, will shine brighter and place everything that is temporary into perspective.

# The Plate Licking Club

## Radhanath & Kilimba

*have been running Radiance Cuisine in San Rafael, California since March 2010. Their love affair with delicious food combined with more than 20 years of international, vegetarian culinary experience is reflected in their passion for creating and serving extraordinary wholesome menus.*

*If you're ever in the Bay Area, make sure to stop by for your own prasadam experience.*

www.radiancecuisine.com

I was chatting with a wonderful couple in Northern California. They make food for customers every day. Their cafe is inside a well-known and much-loved bookshop. Due to the internet revolution, it is harder for independent bookshops to survive. The extra income generated from the cafe helps to ensure its survival.

They were telling me how they often do long and very physical twelve-hour days. At the end of such a day, they told me, it was the "Plate-licking Club" that sustained them. I asked what this was. Well, the prasadam we make fills some people with such joy that some of them have actually licked their plates. Others have said they would "love to lick their plates, it was so delicious". So, over the years, we have taken pictures of our "plate-licking customers" in our minds and we have dozens of them memorized in our hearts. It is a boost to recall this feeling when we want to remember why we are doing what we are doing!

You can find some of their "award winning" recipes on the pages that follow.

"...the prasadam we serve fills some people with such joy that they can't help themselves licking their plate."

AR AS SUSTAINABLY POSSIBLE,
ORGANIC
CAL & SEASONAL
PRODUCE
ARE USED

BOWL SM / LG
ombination of:
AIN · VEGGIES .... 8. / 11.

KS★
WATER OR SODA .... 2.
NIC TEAS ...... 2.50
D ORGANIC 12oz / 16oz
OOLER ....... 3. / 4.50

ACOOKIE ..... 4.

ERTS
LADDU ..... 2.75
MAPLE-SWEETENED ORGANIC

# The famous Yogi Bowl

Radiance Cuisine -
Divinely inspired
California cuisine, using
local organic seasonal
produce to create the
freshest most exciting and
emotionally nourishing
dining experience.

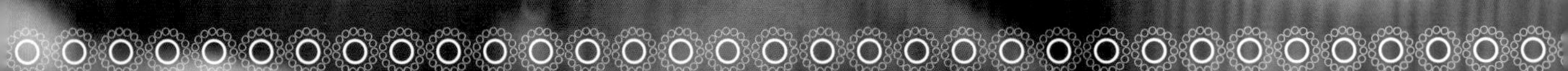

# California Black Bean Soup

Serves 4 - preparation & cooking time 45 minutes

IT'S IMPORTANT TO USE THE FRESHEST LOCAL ORGANIC INGREDIENTS, HERBS, AND PRODUCE, PERHAPS FROM YOUR OWN GARDEN.

## All you need is

- 14 oz (400 gr) cooked organic black beans
- 2 cups (480 ml) of water that beans and 1 bay leaf were cooked in
- 4 tbsp (60 ml) coconut oil
- 1 tsp (5 ml) freshly ground cumin
- 1 tsp (5 ml) chili flakes
- 1/2 tsp (2.5 ml) asafoetida
- 1/2 tsp (2.5 ml) black pepper
- 1 tbsp (15 ml) paprika powder
- 1 medium size turnip* (1 cup or 150 gr) peeled and cut into 1/2 inch (1cm) cubes
- 3 small parsnips* (1 cup or 150 gr) peeled then cut into 1/2 inch (1cm) pieces
- 1 sweet potato* (1 cup or 150 gr) peeled and cut into 1/2 inch (1cm) cubes
- 1/2 tsp (2.5 ml) Himalayan salt
- 2 celery stalks cut into 1/4 inch (5mm) strips and finely diced
- 4 medium size tomatoes blanched, peeled and chopped1/2 inch (1cm) pieces
- 1 tsp (5 ml) coconut sugar or palm sugar
- 8 leaves of rainbow chard or kale leaves finely minced
- 1 tbsp (15 ml) finely chopped fresh cilantro (coriander)
- 1 tbsp (15 ml) finely chopped fresh parsley
- 1 tbsp (15 ml) finely chopped fresh oregano

by Jerry 'Radhanath' Alvarez

## The way

1. In a heavy-bottom big pot, place oil and heat on medium high.

2. When oil is hot, add cumin, chili flakes and asafoetida. Stir gently to lightly brown spices and bring out their aroma (less than a minute). When spices are sizzling and fully fragrant add turnip, potatoes, parsnips and salt, stir to fully coat the vegetables.

3. Let the vegetables brown and get slightly crusty in the spices and oil.

4. Add celery, paprika and black pepper and let cook a bit longer until the veggies are almost cooked.

5. Add tomatoes, sugar and half of the fresh herbs. Stir, lower heat and let cook with the lid on the pot for a few minutes to fully incorporate the flavors.

6. When the tomatoes start to stick to the bottom of the pan, stir and pour in the black beans, water and bay leaf. Add remaining herbs and adjust salt and pepper if needed and serve.

* You may substitute turnip, parsnip and sweet potato with any squash or root vegetable.

# Seasonal Vegetables in Tahini-Cashew Curry Sauce

Serves 4 - preparation and cooking time 1 1/2 hours

### For big pot blanching* vegetables

Use whatever vegetables that are in season and grown locally for best result.

- 1/2 lb (225 gr) broccoli cut into small flowerettes
- 1/2 lb (225 gr) cauliflower cut into small flowerettes
- 1/2 lb (225 gr) butternut squash cut into 1/2 inch (1 cm) cubes
- 1/2 lb (225 gr) Satsuma yam or summer squash cut into 1/2 inch (1 cm) cubes
- 1 gallon (4 liters) filtered water
- 1 cup (240 gr) sea salt

*** Big pot blanching...**
*is a well-known French cooking technique that gives vivid color and the best flavour. The salt in the rapidly boiling water will keep the flavor of the vegetables from leaching into the water and simultaneously season the vegetables perfectly.*

by Jerry 'Radhanath' Alvarez

### The way

1. In a big pot, boil filtered water.
2. Add sea salt.
3. Carefully cook each batch of vegetables separately and be attentive as they each cook differently. You want vegetables cooked 'al dente', bright in color and not over cooked. Make sure the water never loses its boil in between each batch of vegetables.
4. When veggies are ready, scoop out and place in ice-cold water to seal the color and stop the cooking.
5. Drain all veggies and set aside in a large bowl. You will end up with a radiant bowl of perfectly cooked and seasoned veggies.
6. Save 1/2 cup (120 ml) salty brine water to add to sauce.

## For Tahini-Cashew Curry Sauce

- 1 cup (240 gr) tahini
- 1/2 cup (80 gr) raw cashews soaked in water for about an hour
- 1/2 cup (120 ml) filtered water (or more to adjust water to desired creamy consistency)
- 2 tbsp (30 ml) coconut oil
- 1 tsp (5 ml) black mustard seeds
- 6 fresh curry leaves (or dried leaves if you are unable to find fresh)
- 1/4 tsp (2.5 ml) asafoetida
- 1 tbsp (15 ml) fresh minced ginger
- 1/2 tsp (2.5 ml) black pepper
- 1/2 tsp (2.5 ml) cayenne powder
- 1/2 tsp (2.5 ml) turmeric
- 1 cup (175 gr) butternut squash pieces
- 1/2 cup (120 ml) salty brine water from vegetables
- 1/2 cup (120 ml) fresh filtered water

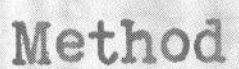

## Method

1. Put tahini, drained and rinsed cashews and water in a powerful blender until smooth to the consistency of cream. Set aside in bowl.
2. Place oil in saucepan over a medium-high heat.
3. When hot add mustard seeds, after they pop add curry leaves then the rest of the spices.
4. When spices are sizzling and fragrant add butternut squash and sauté until browned and crusty.
5. Add salty brine water plus fresh water to pot and cook until squash is tender.
6. Blend all ingredients in blender until smooth to the consistency of cream.
7. Pour through a fine strainer to smooth out the curry sauce. Add curry sauce to the tahini-cashew cream and mix well. Test and adjust for flavor and saltiness.
8. Lavishly pour over veggies and mix together. Serve warm.

# Steamed Quinoa with Sage, Roasted Pumpkin Seeds & Currants

**Serves 4 - preparation + cooking time 25 minutes**

### All you need is...

- 1 1/2 cups (255 gr) organic quinoa
- 3 cups (720 ml) filtered water
- 1 tsp (5 ml) Himalayan salt
- 2 tsp (10 ml) coconut oil
- 4 - 8 fresh sage leaves
- 2 tbsp (20 gr) raw pumpkin seeds
- 2 tbsp (20 gr) dried currants
- pinch of Himalayan salt

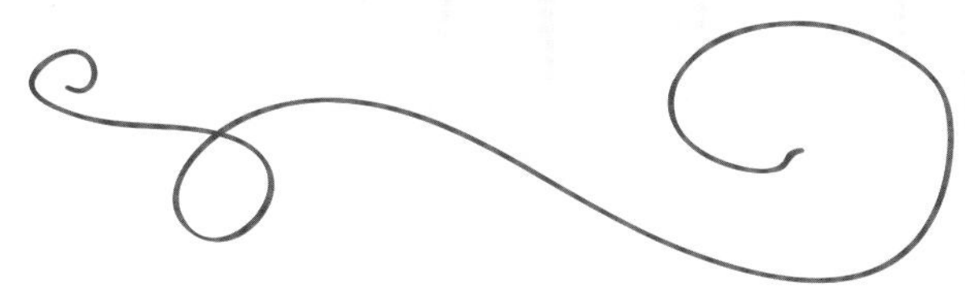

### The way

Steam quinoa in a rice cooker or small pot, the way you would cook rice.

1. Bring water to boil, add 1 tsp salt and then add quinoa.
2. Let simmer and cover pot with lid and cook for 20 minutes.
3. A few minutes before you are ready to serve or while the quinoa is cooking, place coconut oil in a small frying pan on medium-high heat and sauté sage leaves until crispy.
4. Add pumpkin seeds, lightly toast them evenly, then add currants and cook until they puff up.
5. Add a pinch of salt and stir.
6. Serve a scoop full of quinoa on individual plates and top with seed and currant mixture. Be sure to decorate each serving with its own crispy sage leaf or two.

by Jerry 'Radhanath' Alvarez

# “Radiance” Seasonal Salad with Creamy Vegan Orange-Parsley Dressing

**Serves 4 - preparation time 1 hour and putting together 15 minutes**

### Salad Ingredients

- Using the best of whatever is fresh, organic and in season!
- All-organic baby-gem lettuces of purple and green; crunchy shaves of purple cabbage and fennel bulb; sliced French breakfast radishes, lightly blanched thin golden beet wedges, and a sprinkling of sliced almonds, dry-toasted with fresh thyme.

### Dressing Ingredients

- 1/4 cup (40 gr) raw sunflower seeds and 1 1/2 tbsp (20 gr) cashews, soaked in filtered water for at least an hour, then drained and rinsed
- Juice from 3 lemons plus the juice from one extra lemon set aside
- Olive oil to match the quantity of juice from the 3 lemons
- Handful of fresh Italian parsley
- 1/4 of an orange including rind (organic)
- 1/2 tsp (2.5 ml) capers
- 1 tsp (5 ml) apple cider vinegar
- 2 dates, chopped
- 1/4 tsp (2.5 ml) Himalayan salt
- 1 tsp (5 ml) agave nectar (or honey)

### Method

1. Put all dressing ingredients, (except the extra lemon and the soaked seeds and cashews) into a powerful blender.
2. Add a cube of ice to keep blender from heating up.
3. When mixture is smooth, add the seeds and nuts, along with 1-2 more ice cubes and the remaining lemon juice.
4. Drizzle dressing abundantly over salad.

by Kilimba G Alvarez

# Goodness

"How do you feel when you drink too much coffee?" I answered, "Wired!" "Yes", he replied and continued...

In 1995 I became friends with an American gentleman who had been exploring bhakti-yoga for twenty-seven years. He patiently answered my questions knowing that another answer would probably lead to a further three questions. I remember there was a philosophical point that I was really attracted to. He explained that money is earned and money is spent. You can never be sure that what is in your bank account will remain intact tomorrow or in a year or ten years. Spiritual credits, on the other hand, are different. If you start to practice spiritual life, then those credits stay with you even if at some point you stop doing anything. Whatever you gained in spiritual terms stays with you. And whenever you start again, even if it is in your next lifetime (the philosophy of bhakti-yoga presupposes reincarnation), you start from wherever you left off.

I was really struck by this. First, as a businessman, it seemed like a really good deal. Building a business and making money can be tough. You can develop a business for years, and sometimes, events outside your control can take it away from you. The spiritual process seemed far more compassionate and set up to maximise your chances.

I asked him what conditions are favourable for progress in bhakti-yoga. He explained that progress in any walk of life requires some dedication and effort. If you want to improve at a sport, gain a qualification or learn a language, you have to undertake certain repetitive tasks. Spiritual life, he explained, was no different.

I asked him to expand on this and share with me his experiences. He explained that one of the greatest books to have emanated from India is called the Bhagavad-Gita. "Bhagavad" means "God, the Supreme Personality of Godhead, who is filled with six opulences (the totality of wealth, strength, fame, knowledge, beauty, and renunciation) " and "Gita" means "song". Literally, the book means "The song of God." He explained that any spiritual philosophy needs to be supported by the ancient scriptures. Even though these scriptures were composed thousands of years ago, they are as relevant today as they were then. The Bhagavad-Gita deals with the fundamental issues that face everyday people.

I asked him for a starting point with regard to the Bhagavad-Gita. Although it is available in English, it originated in the ancient Indian language of Sanskrit. So I was a bit intimidated but highly curious about this book. I wanted him to help create a bridge for me to develop a relationship with the Bhagavad-Gita.

He asked me: "How do you feel when you drink too much coffee?"

I answered: "Wired!"

"Yes", he replied. "How about when you drink alcohol and possibly get drunk?"

"Sometimes I feel jolly for a while," I replied, "but sooner or later I crash and feel dehydrated and have pain in my head."

"I will show you how these things can impede spiritual progress. Anyone who wants to get really good at anything has to give something up. To do well at exams you give up time to do so. To become a great sports-person you regulate your diet."

He went to explain the core teaching of the Bhagavad-Gita. "In this material world, there are only three things in existence," he started. "First, there is God, or Krishna. Second, there are an infinite number of living entities or souls. And, third, there are inanimate objects. It's that simple."

After a moment to reflect, he explained, "The highest love that exists anywhere in the spiritual or material world is the love of God. There is a level of love of God that exists that is so sublime and so powerful that your temporary human body could not continue to exist if filled with it. You would have to go back to the spiritual world to maintain that level of love." This really intrigued me and made some kind of sense. At this point I was not trying to understand everything with my head. I was engaging my heart and taking it all in like you would take in a work of art or a poem.

"Love is voluntary. If it is not voluntary, then it is not love," he said.

"Yes, this is true in any terms; everyday relationships too."

Seeing that I was comfortable with the philosophy, he went further: "This is why everything is set up whereby we can love from an extraordinary extent at one end of the spectrum to nothing at all at the other end." I thought about this. So what he is saying is that if The Supreme Personality of Godhead does not give us the free will to forget Him entirely, then the highest love would not be possible.

I wanted to know more. "So how do we climb this ladder of love, then?" I asked. "The first step," he said, holding the Bhagavad-Gita, "is to try to live in good energy."

"What does that mean?" I thought. It felt a bit abstract and too vague. However, the rest of his explanation was clear and rational.

"You see, in the Bhagavad-Gita, there is a great personality, Arjuna. Arjuna is a warrior and a lover of God. He faces a battle he does not wish to fight. He is on his chariot and his driver is Krishna Himself. The Personality of Godhead is personally driving his chariot. This is very beautiful. It shows how the Supreme Lord can be controlled by the love of His friend. He is willing to take the inferior role of the chariot driver. Devotion is sublime."

He paused and closed his eyes for a couple of seconds as if ingesting some of this mood. He continued: "This exchange between Krishna and Arjuna is very beautiful, and the whole Bhagavad-Gita is derived from Krishna answering Arjuna's sixteen questions.

"But now imagine a totally separate chariot, and it is an excellent metaphor. The chariot is the body. The passenger is the soul. The driver is the intelligence, the reins are the mind, and the fives horses are the senses—namely, taste, touch, smell, sight and sound. The goal of life is to become a lover of God. This potential exists already within your soul. This is a sublime and gentle process that requires self-awareness and humility. If we are continually over-stimulated through our senses—drinking, taking drugs [or drug addiction], smoking and so on—then our mind cannot be steady and our soul remains covered. The potential of the soul remains unchanged. In the same way, if the reins do not control the horses, then the driver will be overwhelmed, the chariot will go off course, and the passenger will not reach the ultimate goal. In fact, he can fall off a cliff."

"So what does this have to do with good energy?" I asked, reminding him of his previous comment.

"This is the key to the door," he said. "The mind is very restless and hard to control. If we have our senses under control, then our mind can be still and we can be better guided by the Lord.. If the mind is disturbed or distracted it is very hard to hear Him whispering to you. There is too much noise."

To conclude the explanation, he said: "The Bhagavad-Gita explains that if someone lives in the mode of goodness, and not passion or ignorance, then the mind can be still and the journey to ever-increasing devotion to Krishna can be simple."

I enquired: "What does this entail?"

"Follow a vegetarian diet. No meat, chicken, fish or eggs, and avoid coffee, tea,alcohol, onions and garlic. This will still your mind and put you in a better condition to feel His love.. The affection, protection, and nourishment is always there. It is up to us to receive it."

"But it is important to progress at your own pace," he added. "This is not about sinning or not sinning and going to heaven or hell. No, it is about the abundance of mercy that is patiently waiting for you to perceive it. So much of this is available. If we could clean the window to the soul, we would feel this mercy, this tenderness shining through. Then we can reach our spiritual potential."

"Ah!" I exclaimed quite excitedly, "It is almost as if we need to get out of our own way, and then the love of God will flow through us. In one way this sounds as easy or as hard as we make it, because you are saying the mercy is there, as if being showered on us from heavy cumulus clouds in the sky. It is up to us to reach out, with big empty buckets in our hearts, ready to receive it. It is there for all."

"Yes," he replied softly and with satisfaction. "You have understood what it is that I am saying. You are also touching on another subject, 'causeless mercy', which is for another day."

There are many people who experience prasadam as a perfect way to build this solid platform for spiritual growth. By taking only what is recommended, this will keep the mind focussed and unwavering. Meanwhile, the process of offering will deepen our heart's connection,, enabling us to receive and imbibe more mercy. It helps to know that it is such a simple process which is repeated daily.

My friend concluded: "It is important to get the balance right in spiritual life. Try too little and you won't see a result. Try too much and you can go too fast and regress. It's a steady application. Gradually, use your intelligence to reduce the stimulants and intoxicants that unsettle your mind. Once you are in the driving seat, your intelligence prevailing over your mind, then you are creating a nice patch of garden soil into which you can start 'growing' your bhakti plant."

# Lemon Ginger Mint Cooler

Serves 4 - preparation time 15 minutes

**All you need is ...**

- 1 cup (240 ml) fresh squeezed lemon juice
- 3 cups (720 ml) filtered water (or more to taste)
- 1/4 cup (60 ml) organic agave nectar*
- 1/2 inch x 1 inch (1 cm x 2.5 cm) fresh ginger, peeled and minced
- 10 mint leaves
- 8 ice cubes

**The way**

1. After squeezing the lemons, pour through a very fine strainer into a medium sized bowl.
2. Put all other ingredients into blender and blend for 30 seconds. Pour contents through the fine strainer into the bowl of fresh lemon juice and whisk together.
3. Strain once more. Add ice. Voila!

* Agave is a natural liquid sweetener. You may substitute with honey.

Recipe by Kilimba G Alvarez

# When life brings you lemons ...

# Saffron-Vanilla Tapioca Pudding

Serves 4 - preparation and cooking time 40 minutes

## All you need is ...

- 1 cup (240 ml) filtered water
- 4 peppercorns
- 1/2 of one fresh bay leaf or 1 medium size dried bay leaf
- 1/2 of one dried vanilla bean, slit or 1/2 teaspoon (2.5 ml) pure vanilla extract
- pinch of pure saffron
- pinch of Himalayan salt
- 14 oz (400 ml) organic, full cream coconut milk
- 2 tbsp (30 ml or 25 gr) granulated tapioca
- 1/4 cup (50 ml) maple syrup

offered by Kilimba G Alvarez

MADE WITH ORGANIC COCONUT MILK AND SWEETENED WITH PURE MAPLE SYRUP

## The way

1. Bring water to a boil in a saucepan.
2. Add peppercorns, bay leaf, vanilla bean (or extract) and salt.
3. Turn heat down to medium and let simmer for 10 minutes with lid on.
4. Add coconut milk and whisk till smooth.
5. Bring to a rolling boil on medium high heat and then add the saffron, turning the strands to powder between your fingers as it sprinkles in.
6. Let simmer on medium heat for 10 minutes.
7. Take out the peppercorns, bay leaf and vanilla bean.
8. Turn heat up to medium-high and when it comes to a rolling boil, sprinkle in the granulated tapioca while whisking continuously for 10 more minutes or until the tapioca becomes translucent and is starting to thicken the pudding.
9. Put in refrigerator to cool.
10. When cooled, whisk in the maple syrup, pour into dessert glasses and keep cool until serving. Serve with tiny spoons for the sheer joy of it.

**Note:** You may also serve warm

# Planet

"Environmental issues were not my strong point and this gentleman clearly knew his facts. I was happy to be the student..."

When I was a child, family meals out meant Chinese meals. So I have always associated Chinese food with happy family occasions. Some time ago I was sitting in my favourite Chinese restaurant in London. It is totally vegetarian with over one hundred scrumptious dishes. Vegetarians do not usually enjoy more than two or three choices off the menu. So, being able to have anything off the menu can in itself be challenging!

I was in early, so there were no other customers present. The waiter and I started to chat. Quite spontaneously, he turned to me and asked, "Did you know that by eating a fully veggie meal you are saving fifty-five square feet of rain forest? Pretty good, eh!" "That's good to know," I replied. After a few more spoonfuls of soup, I added, "I have been a vegetarian for over twenty years but, to be honest, the decision was not ecologically driven."

It is a friendly kind of restaurant and I was in an open and communicative mood. The waiter must have picked up on this as he sat down and looked at me quite intensely and said, "Our planet is crying out for us all to become vegetarians. Planet Earth is groaning with the pain and violence being inflicted on it by a rising human population.

It is more grave than this. Incomes are rising and fashions are changing. This means each person is eating more and there are so many more people. Even putting aside arguments about whether we are herbivores, carnivores or omnivores, it is evident that this modern period is unique because in previous times most people ate meat occasionally. They couldn't afford to eat meat every day."

I was a bit out of my depth. Environmental issues were not my strong point and this gentleman clearly knew his facts. I was happy to be the student. Without my needing to prompt him, he furthered his argument. "Food production is highly water intensive. And meat production takes much more water than vegetarian food production. The meal you are having now has saved the planet 2,400 gallons. Given that most political commentators say that the most precious resource of the 21st century will be water as well as oil, this is a serious issue."

I found his arguments compelling, and the numbers were quite startling. I did not realise that he had given me just the hors d'oevres of facts. Far more shocking numbers were to follow.

"Do you think more land is needed to produce the equivalent amount of a meat-based diet or a vegetarian diet?" he asked.

"Clearly meat is more land-intensive," I responded confidently.

"Yes, by how many times do you think?" he asked searchingly.

"Three or five times," I guessed.

"No," he said, "twenty times." That is a huge difference, I thought.

I ordered my main course. The waiter disappeared into the kitchen. I started to glance through a pamphlet on vegetarianism that the restaurant produces. It explained that since the 1990s, 90% of all deforestation of the Amazon has been for clearing land for cattle grazing. Another extraordinary statistic that struck me is that every minute the equivalent of seven football fields are cleared for farmland to feed the livestock of the meat industry. In the United States, 260 million acres of forest has been cleared for this farming, and furthermore 30% of the Earth's land-mass has been turned to agriculture. These massive numbers are due to man's non-vegetarian diet.

It was still early, and by the time my main course came in, there were a couple more customers in the restaurant. As the staff still outnumbered the customers, my waiter felt able to continue chatting with me.

I thought that I would take the lead. "Has anyone estimated what percentage of global warming is caused by the meat industry?"

"Yes," he replied. "What is your gut feel?"

I had absolutely no idea but I figured that global warming must be mainly due to cars and airplanes. "7%," I gambled.

"You're going to be very surprised. Double that. And then double it again and almost again! 51%."

"Who produced that number?" I asked sceptically, to which he shot back without hesitation, "Worldwatch."

He could see I was taken aback. Normally

I eat there with a voracious appetite, but by now I was just playing around with my food. “People have no idea,” he said. “We are going about shopping at our local supermarket, doing what everyone else does. And because everyone else does it, it’s okay. I reckon this will be as shocking a concept to people in two hundred years’ time, as we find slavery today when we judge our ancestors. To land a kilo of beef into someone’s fridge causes 36.4kg of $CO_2$. That’s about the equivalent of a 250 kilometre car journey for the average European. We don’t realise just how much grain we have to provide these animals to end up with the flesh that we consume. It’s massive and it’s inefficient.”

This really opened my eyes. I suddenly realised how much went into meat-eating. The animals are reared and fed. They digest and excrete and are highly flatulent. They are killed and stored and transported. It’s an enormous undertaking. And then there is all the deforestation. We are not just harming the planet. It is a multiple attack, I thought, like a crazed knifeman slashing his victim multiple times.

“Here is another statistic to keep you up at night,” my waiter chided. “To produce a single calorie of animal protein will cause eleven times as much $CO_2$ to be released as a single calorie of plant protein.”

“Staggering!” I thought. At this point I was suffering more from indigestion of information than food. I thought, perhaps, he had reached a peak. However, there was still more to come.

“You know”, he continued, “methane is an even bigger danger than $CO_2$. Did you know that a pound of methane traps twenty times the amount of heat in our atmosphere as $CO_2$? With billions of animals in the process of being grown, reared and killed, methane is produced from flatulence and faeces. Due to meat mass production, there are so many animals on the planet that in the United States they produce more excrement than the whole of humanity. This equates to 89,000 pounds per second. All of this happens without proper treatment systems.” He paused, asking me if I wanted anything else to eat.

“No,” I replied. “This information is staggering. To be honest, I am finding it hard to eat and absorb this information at the same time.”

“Sure,” he said, “when you first hear this stuff, it is confronting. Fundamentally, eating animals on the scale that we do is highly inefficient. In 1993, for example, 192.7 million tons of grain and feed were consumed by US farm animals. This produced 31.2 million tons of meat. The difference was spent on moving, excreting and flatulence. That's a lot of numbers, I know! In other words, for every six kilos of grain and feed consumed by animals, less than one kilo of meat was produced."

Live Earth, the anti-global warming concerts helped by Al Gore, says that not eating meat is the "single most effective thing you can do to reduce your climate change impact."

This conversation really opened my eyes to the destruction that is being wrought by modern habits of meat eating.

# THE GARDEN OF GOD

One of my favourite stories involves a family who live in Birmingham, England. They take the idea of offering their food to God one step further. They have their own allotments and they buy the seed and offer the seed to God first. What ends up on their table is prasadam that has been fully offered to God from the soil to the seed to the cultivation to the harvest, preparation and consumption.

These vegetables, they tell me, almost bounce into their mouths. They have so much energy!

*Sarojini's joy of cooking extends over years of working as a chef, caterer and supplier for whole food shops and cafes. Nandasuta finds his bliss is in hosting and cooking for spiritual festivals. They are both inventive chefs at home with their children and share a passion to cook for Krishna. Visit Sarojini's blog, "The Yogi Vegetarian", filled with divinely inspired recipes and information about eating holistically and healthily, the Bhakti Yoga way.*

**Read her blog on** www.kitchenoflove.com

# Avocado + Sprout Salad

## with lime and cumin dressing

Serves 4 - preparation and cooking time 15 minutes

**All you need is**

- 2 ripe (but not squishy) avocados
- The juice of 4 small limes
- 1 tbsp (15 ml) extra-virgin olive oil
- 1 1/2 tsps (7.5 ml) cumin seeds
- A pinch of sea salt
- 1/4 tsp (1.25 ml) coarse-ground black pepper
- 4 heaped tbsp (60 gr) mixed sprouts (alfalfa with chickpea, mung and aduki sprouts)

**The way**

1. First, dry-roast the cumin seeds over a medium heat in a sturdy-bottomed pan, stirring until they begin to release their aroma. Remove from heat and set aside.

2. Combine the cumin seeds with the oil, lime juice, salt and pepper in a lidded jar. With the lid on tight (!) shake it until thoroughly combined.

3. Cut and fan out half an avocado for each person, on a bed of sprouts of your choice.

4. Pour about a tablespoon of dressing onto each avocado, according to your taste.

Recipe by Sarojini dasi

**Tip:** You can also use tofu, sweet corn, fresh coriander or parsley, or return to this dish's Indian roots and spice with roasted cumin seeds, fresh fenugreek, chili or ginger. You can use pretty much anything you have to hand; there's so much scope for imagination and you can make it differently every time if you like!

by Nandasuta das & Sarojini dasi

**The way**

1. Prepare and cut the vegetables.
2. Mix the flour, baking powder and seasonings in a large shallow bowl.
3. Add the water and mix well with a balloon whisk.
4. Heat the oil in a frying pan and drop in 1/4 of the mixture at a time. As with regular pancakes, make sure it does not stick.
5. Add the toppings and cook over a medium to high heat until bottom is cooked. (You will know because the edges will look brown underneath when you lift them up.)
6. Put the pan under a preheated grill until top is set and starting to brown. Or flip over the pancake in the same pan and sprinkle vegan or dairy cheese over the top and let cook until bottom is browned.

# Savoury Gram Flour Pancake

# Pudla

Serves 4 - preparation and cooking time 30 minutes

**ALL YOU NEED**

- 3 cups (300 gr) besan (gram/chickpea) flour
- 4 tsp (20 ml) baking powder
- 1 3/4 cup (400 ml) water
- 1/2 tsp (5 ml) turmeric
- 1/2 tsp (2.5 ml) asafoetida
- 1/2 tsp (2.5 ml) paprika
- 1 tsp (5 ml) mixed fresh or dried herbs of your choice (herbs de Provence/ Italian etc.)
- 1/2 tsp black pepper (or to taste)
- 1 tsp sea salt (or to taste)
- Olive oil for frying
- A selection of toppings: chopped vegetables such as bell peppers, cherry tomatoes, zucchini or any other of your choice
- Vegan or dairy cheese for sprinkling on top

# Pesto Pasta

**Serves 4 - preparation time 10 minutes**

**The way**

1. Cook your favorite pasta.
2. Whizz up the fresh basil with the olive oil in a blender until it forms an oily paste. Add the dried basil, salt, asafoetida, and pine nuts (leaving some whole, then you get little bites of intense pine-nutty flavour in your pesto).
3. Mix in a bowl with the Parmesan and put over your cooked pasta.

Tip: You can also use it as a salad dressing or for cold pasta too.

Recipe by Sarojini dasi

**All you need is**

- 2 oz (50 gr) pine nuts (pignolia)
- 2 oz (50 gr) fresh basil, stalks and all
- 1 tsp (5 ml) dried basil
- 3-4 tbsp (45-60 ml) nice, fruity extra-virgin olive oil
- 1/2 cup vegan or dairy Parmesan cheese coarsely grated
- A pinch of sea salt
- 1 tsp (5 ml) asafoetida
- 1/4 -1/2 tsp (1.2-2.5 ml) coarse-ground black pepper

# Spicy Bean Burgers

## All you need is

- 8.8 oz (250 gr) cooked and mashed red kidney beans
- A handful of each: ground sunflower seeds, ground pumpkin seeds, and ground almonds (first dry pan-roast the seeds and then grind them)
- A handful of grated sweet potato
- 1/2 red bell pepper grated
- 1/4 cup porridge oats
- 1/2 tbsp (7.5ml) sesame seeds
- 1.7 oz (50 gr) tomato puree
- 1/2 tbsp (7.5 ml) soy sauce
- 1/2 tsp (2.5 ml) asafoetida
- 11/2 tsp (7.5 ml) chilli powder (or according to taste)
- 1 1/2 tsp (7.5 ml) paprika powder
- 1 tbsp (15 ml) dried herbs de Provence (thyme, oregano, basil, etc.)

**Serves 4 -**
**preparation time 15 minute,**
**cooking time 25-30 minutes**

## THE WAY

1. Combine dry ingredients and mix well.
2. Add grated vegetables, then seasonings.
3. Roll into 4 balls and place on an oiled baking tray, pressing them into burger shapes with a spatula.
4. Bake at 400°F (200°C) until browned slightly (about 20 minutes), turning halfway through. You can also grill or shallow fry them after you have baked them for a little crispy edge, but don't cook them too long or they dry out.
5. Serve in a wholemeal bun with a fresh green salad and or avocado & sprout salad, and spicy potato wedges.

**Tip:** Add your favourite vegan or dairy cheese

by Sarojini dasi

# Gingery Rhubarb Apple Crumble

Serves 4 – preparation time 15 minutes, cooking time 15–20 minutes

## All you need for crumble filling

- 4 or 5 sticks of rhubarb, sliced into 1 inch (2.5 cm) pieces
- 1 apple cut into 1 inch (2.5 cm) pieces
- 3 tbsp (45 ml) raw cane sugar (or to taste)

## Topping ingredients

- 1/2 cup jumbo oats
- 1/2 cup porridge oats, ground a little finer
- 1/2 cup ground almonds
- 1/2 cup ground pumpkin seeds
- 1/2 cup hemp flour (or whole wheat flour)
- 1 cup raw cane sugar
- 2 tsp (10 ml) powdered ginger (or to taste)
- 2 tbsp (30 ml) extra-virgin olive oil (or more if desired)

## Method

1. Heat the rhubarb pieces, apple and the raw cane sugar in a pan until soft. (Add enough sugar so that the rhubarb does not taste too tart.) Strain off any excess juice and save for adding to the crumble topping.

2. Mix all the topping ingredients together in a large bowl then rub in olive oil.

3. Mix in cooked fruit juice, just enough for the mixture to stick together.

4. Put fruit in a heatproof baking dish and spread the topping over it, evenly.

5. Bake in a pre-heated oven at 400°F (200°C) until the top is just starting to brown, 15-20 minutes.

* You can use a food processor or electric grinder for this. This is optional.

**Tip:** This crumble is delicious served with custard made from soya milk or dairy milk and custard powder.

offered by Sarojini dasi

# Banana + Pineapple Smoothie

Serves 4 - preparation time 5 minutes

All you need is...

- 4 ripe bananas
- 2 cups (480 ml) milk or soya milk
- 2 round slices of fresh pineapple, peeled
- 4 tbsp (60 ml) natural
  bio yoghurt / soya yoghurt

The way ...

1. Chop banana and pineapple.
2. Whizz all ingredients in a blender until thoroughly combined.
3. Add more milk to thin the liquid, if too thick.

offered by Tamal Krishna ji

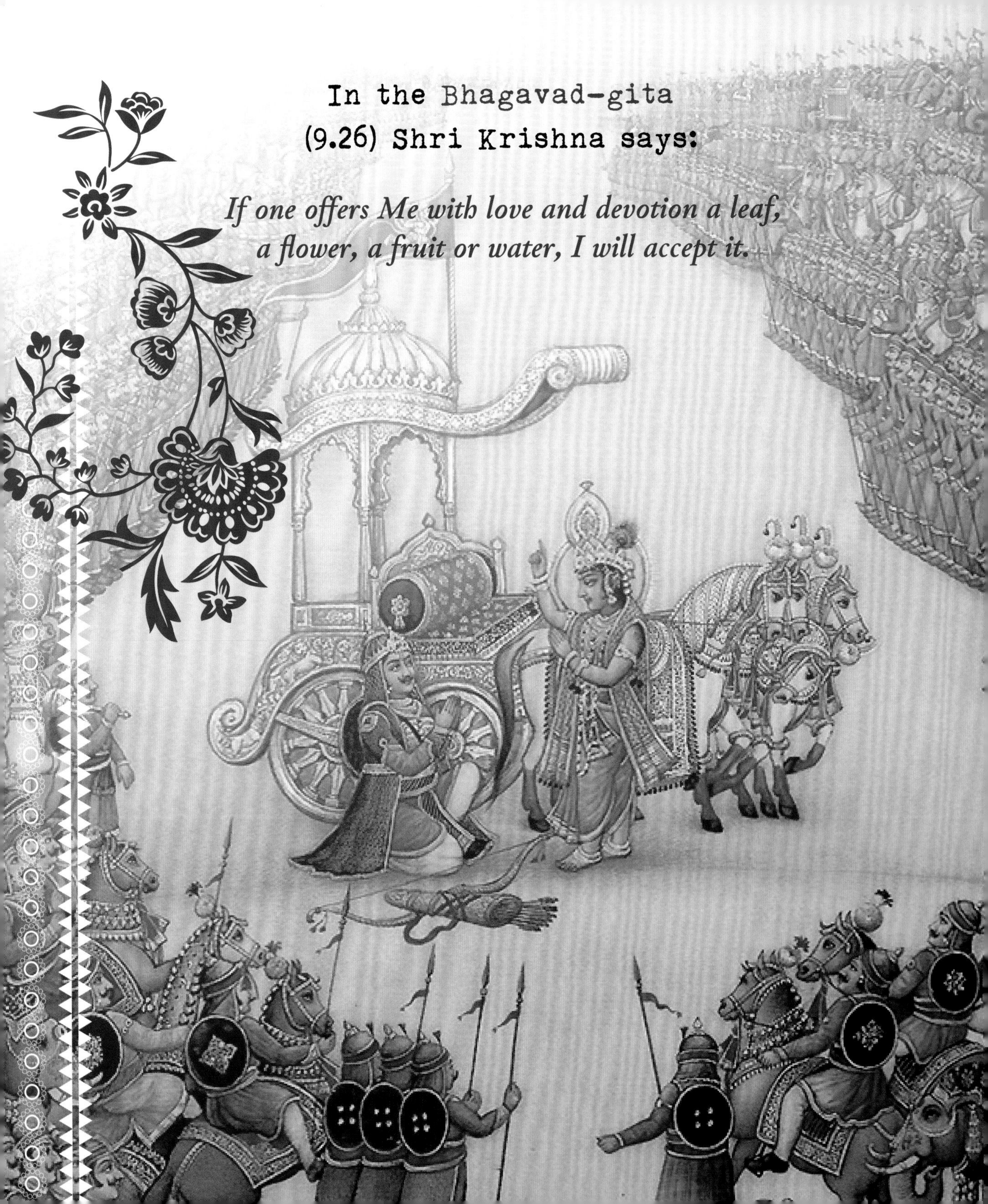

In the Bhagavad-gita
(9.26) Shri Krishna says:

*If one offers Me with love and devotion a leaf,*
*a flower, a fruit or water, I will accept it.*

We have nothing to offer Krishna because He is the Proprietor of everything that be. But when He sees that a living entity is trying to serve Him, that is appreciated. In Bhagavad-gita you have seen that Krishna says to offer Him a leaf, a fruit, a flower or even some water. Actually, the Supreme Lord has no necessity to request us to offer Him these items or any other items; but He gives us the opportunity of serving Him so that we may become qualified to enter back to Home, back to Godhead.

AC Bhaktivedanta Swami Srila Prabhupada

# Wellness

"I looked around the room. It was somewhat expressionless but he definitely had everyone's attention."

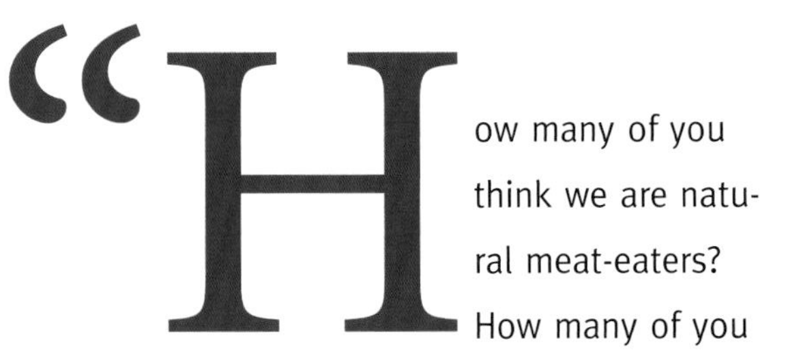

ow many of you think we are natural meat-eaters? How many of you think we are designed to eat everything? How many of you think we are natural vegetarians?" asked the seminar leader.

Most of the attendees stuck up their hand for the first two choices. One person voted for "vegetarian". Even though I am a vegetarian, I opted for "everything".

"You are all victims of 'the meat delusion'. Somehow modern man has convinced himself that we are natural meat-eaters, even though every biological and anthropological fact supports the idea that we are natural vegetarians."

I sensed the room getting tense. I was in a detox centre in Europe. Folks from many countries and walks of life spend a week or two on a strict regime. The idea is to abstain from eating, take some vitamin pills and juices and thin soup, and do some light exercise daily such as yoga. Your system gets a good clean-out and you bounce out of there with energy. However, the detox centre is also keen to educate its customers on the human body and nutrition, and to change some misconceptions.

"We eat meat today because we can. Prior to refrigeration, it was just not possible to consume so much meat. And people were a lot poorer, so meat was available to the rich, not the poor."

Our teacher became silent and studied the room. I could see he was used to facing rooms of people who did not agree with him. He was a man at ease with himself. This meant that the tension in the room remained with the subject matter and did not become personal. I got the sense from him that he would like to persuade us to his way of thinking. However, he was mature enough to be relaxed if you did not.

"This morning, I am going to demonstrate to you two things. One is that humans have been designed to be vegetarians. Two is that being vegetarian is healthy and promotes longevity."

I looked around the room. It was somewhat expressionless, but he definitely had everyone's attention.

"Don't believe me. Believe the experts," he continued with a slightly raised voice. "In a report called 'The China Study', Dr T. Colin Campbell gives a lot of evidence that we were vegetarian well before we started to eat meat." The teacher continued: "Then there's Dr Neal Barnard, who wrote 'The Power of Your Plate'. He tells us: 'You can't tear flesh by hand, you can't tear hide by hand. We wouldn't have been able to deal with food sources that required those large canines.' Although we have teeth called canines, they bear little resemblance to the canines of carnivores."

He placed his papers on his desk and then slowly collected another pile of papers. He was letting the information seep in, to be absorbed by our consciousness. "Here's another expert," he started up again. "Dr William C. Roberts makes the point that while we kill animals to eat them, they kill us through the diseases we suffer from meat eating."

He then sat on the chair in front of us and leaning forward pleaded, "Ladies and gentlemen, these are top nutritional and anthropological scientists reporting objectively on what they see in front of them. They are not lobbyists, advertisers or biased."

You could feel the room shift. We were hearing well-reasoned arguments. Our speaker commanded the respect of the room.

"Are you ready for some good news?" He asked. At least five hands went up and a few others shouted "yes" or "yeah". "Well the good news," he said, confident his audience was awake and engaged, "is that this is not quantum physics. You don't have to be an expert to observe the obvious."

He then went to his whiteboard and started drawing a human body on the left-hand side and a cat on the right-hand side. Within each body he drew lines that started at the mouth and finished at the base of the spine.

"Intestines," he exclaimed, tapping at the board with his pen. "Meat-eating animals have short intestines, enabling them to absorb the nutrients while discarding the rotten flesh quickly. Vegetarian animals have much longer intestines. The intestinal tract of meat-eating animals does not exceed three times the length of their bodies. Human beings have tracts at six times the length of their body."

A hand went up. Hamdy was a fifty-something Egyptian. He was well read, had travelled and ran a meat factory. "This is just one aspect of the human body," Hamdy asserted. "Your presentation is powerful, but narrowly based." Hamdy looked quite pleased with himself. He wasn't someone easily convinced. Our speaker was not phased. "I have only just begun," he quipped. "I can show you at least six self-evident facts relating to meat-eating animals on the one hand and humans on the other that point in the same direction." Hamdy looked genuinely fascinated.

"Let's look at the claws." Our speaker was picking up speed. It was as if he could see the end in sight. He could sense the conversion of his audience was within his grasp. "Meat-eating animals have claws. Vegetarian animals do not have claws. Ladies and gentlemen, please turn to the person next two you and show them your hands. Then please ask each other if you see any claws." Everyone laughed and carried out this comical exercise. He then asked, "How many people saw claws? Hands up please." No hands went up and an air of frivolity permeated the group.

"Turn to each other again, please. Stick out your tongues. Observe your partner's tongue. Does it perspire like a dog's tongue? You see, animal meat-eaters' tongues perspire. Vegetarian animals' tongues do not perspire." This was a hilarious exercise. For fun, Hamdy insisted that his partner's tongue did perspire. "Meat-eating animals do not have skin pores. Like all other vegetarian animals, humans have skin pores." I felt the arguments of the speaker becoming irresistible.

"The same applies to our teeth. Meat-eaters have sharp front teeth for tearing flesh. They have no flat molars for grinding. For vegetarian animals including humans, the front teeth are blunt and the molars are flat."

He stroked his chin and paused before adding, "Often people tell me that we humans must be natural meat-eaters because of our canine teeth. But this is classic word confusion. We get confused by our own terminology. They are called 'canine' because of their relative position in the mouth. They have no resemblance to those teeth found in dogs, cats or bears."

He went back to his desk again and fumbled around for a book. He opened it at a pre-marked page: "Let us benefit from another expert, French naturalist Baron Cuvier, who wrote: 'Fruits, roots, and the succulent parts of vegetables appear to be the natural food of man: his hands afford him a facility in gathering them; and his short and comparatively weak jaws, his short canine not passing beyond the common line of others, and the tuberculous teeth, would not permit him to devour flesh."

The seminar leader smiled and continued, "Look at the respective stomachs. Meat-eating animals and vegetarian animals have stomachs that contain hydrochloric acid. The meat-eating animals contain stronger acid. How much stronger do you think the acid is?"

The general consensus was somewhere between two and five. "Twenty times," our speaker shot back.

"In all vegetarian animals including humans, we have well-developed salivary glands to pre-digest grains and fruit. Meat-eating animals do not have these. Meat-eating animals tend to have powerful jaws and long fangs. Other than a certain gentleman from Transylvania, we do not."

Everyone sensed the seminar drawing to a close. "Convinced?" our speaker cheekily enquired. "And I haven't even touched on health yet. Meat-eating leads to more heart disease, higher blood pressure, more kidney disease and causes sickness due to bacteria."

"Who will now consider that humans may be vegetarian?" Everyone raised his hand. "How many of you are convinced that we are natural vegetarians?" Out of twenty attendees, fourteen agreed with him.

# Holy Cow

"Mother of deep pearly wisdom,
Mother of a thousand rivers of milk..."

Poem to the "cows of Goloka Vrindavana"

# Holy Cow

Eyelashed beauty
Innocent as the moon's glow
Sublime as the pre-dawn
Auspiciousness and sweetness

A mood like no other
Never does she ask for a blade of grass
Yet she gives herself untold times
She is sacrifice, mercy, mother

In you all healing
Within you all mercy
From you all goodness
With you grace

You who smells of deep sweetness
You who chews nonchalantly
You who personifies passivity
You who are tolerance incarnate

You are of the celestial plane
The Lord holds you dear
Pleasing all
You carry the gift of life

Mother of deep pearly wisdom
Mother of a thousand rivers of milk
Mother of sweet Earth
Mother we honour your grace

You bestow mercy
Incarnate compassion
You are abundance
And all good fortune

Your sway is ease itself
You chew like Time has ceased
Pretty eyelashes melt my heart
Sink me into your soul

Your gait God's grace
Your smell celestial
Your eyes pure innocence
Your skin pure healing

# The Guru & the Muffin

"My Guru collected hearts for Krishna like a florist collects flowers for a wonderful bouquet."

Bhakti-yoga is an ancient method that helps us evolve so that we may become pure lovers of God. The word Guru comes from two words: gu means darkness and ru means light. The Guru leads us from the darkness to the light.

A question that is often asked of me is, "How do you know your Guru is qualified to be Guru?" There are many attributes of a Guru. One of the ones I like very much is that the best Guru is the best disciple. My Guru had his own Guru. Gurudeva showed by all accounts that he is a very dedicated servant to his Guru.

Gurudeva made his divine appearance in this world in 1921 in the state of Bihar. He was such a knowledgeable person on all matters regarding the scriptures and bhakti-yoga. What made him extraordinary, however, was how self-evidently loving he was. It oozed from him.

Neither of my parents believe in God. When my father was in hospital I took him a book. He rustled through the preliminary pages. When he arrived at the photograph of Gurudeva he stopped and pointed with vigour at him exclaiming, "He's the one for me!" He didn't even believe in God!

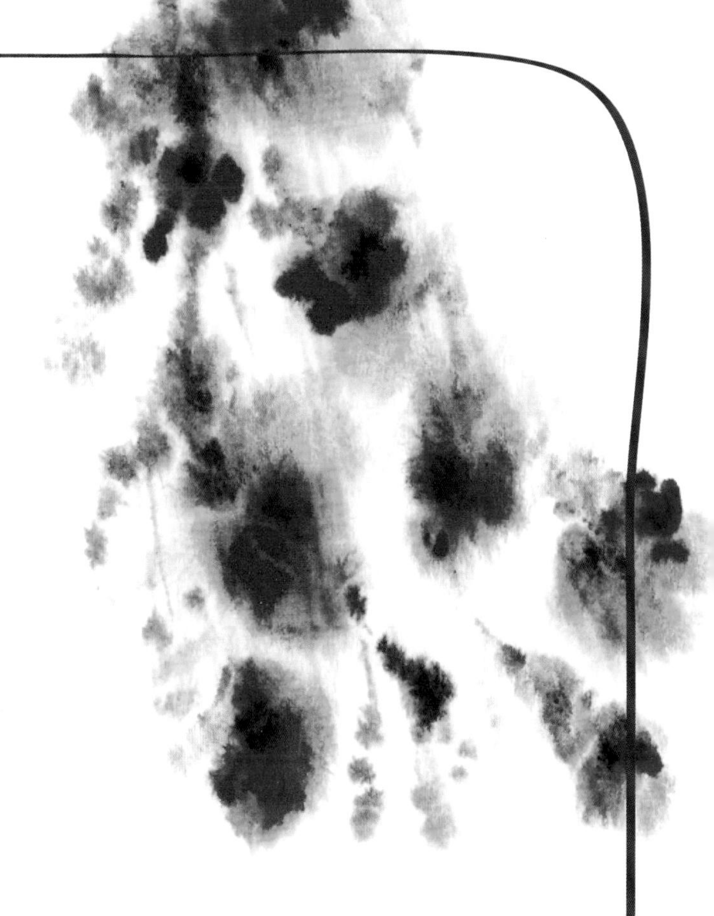

Gurudeva collected hearts for Krishna like a florist collects flowers for a wonderful bouquet. He travelled all over India for years doing so, and then the whole globe from the age of seventy-six until he left the vision of the planet aged ninety. Everywhere he went, he was faithfully served by Madhava Maharaj, one of the monks he had trained. Madhava Maharaj was like a mother to Gurudeva. He cooked for him. Wherever Gurudeva was, Madhava Maharaj was nearby, always serving him. He was always at his side.

As Gurudeva travelled, he attracted more and more followers. Madhava Maharaj had to manage access to him; otherwise Gurudeva could not have written all the wonderful books he did. .

It is traditional that when someone meets a Guru, he or she makes an offering. It may be a flower. It may be fruit. It could be a monetary donation.One day, a disciple came and offered Gurudeva a muffin. Sometimes Madhava Maharaj had to be quite firm. He explained in Hindi that he was not to eat the muffin because it was not appropriate for his diet.

That night, Madhava Maharaj was taking the tray on which the muffin had sat into the kitchen. He picked up the muffin and realised that Gurudeva had dug a hole underneath the muffin and eaten as much of it as he could without the outer part collapsing. Even though Madhava Maharaj had disallowed it, Gurudeva felt compelled to honour the muffin which the disciple had so affectionately prepared. Madhava Maharaj smiled. Love will flow around and over all obstacles. Gurudeva was not going to let a few dietary rules get in the way of him accepting a disciple's offering of love.

## All you need is

- 2 cups (250 gr) flour
- 1 tsp (5 ml) baking soda
- 1 tsp (5 ml) baking powder
- 3/4 cup (125 gr) caster sugar (superfine granulated)
- 1/2 cup (120 gr) butter at room temperature
- 1 tsp (5 ml) vanilla essence
- 3 tbsp (45 ml) milk
- 1 tbsp (15 ml) sour cream
- 3 very ripe medium size bananas
- 1/2 cup of walnuts (optional)

# Priya's Banana Bread

**Preparation and cooking time 1 hour**

## Method

1. Preheat oven 325°F (165°C) (or 320°F or 160°C if fan-forced). Grease a loaf tin, line base with baking paper.
2. Beat butter and sugar in a large bowl with an electric mixer until light and fluffy.
3. Add milk, sour cream and vanilla essence and mix well.
4. In a separate bowl, mash bananas then add to mixture.
5. Sift in flour, baking soda and baking powder and mix with a wooden spoon. Add nuts and mix well (optional).
6. Pour mixture into tin and bake about 45-50 minutes (ovens may vary).
7. Cool on wire rack.

**Tip:** For a fun alternative, make banana muffins, in a twelve-muffin tin and pre-heated oven at 350°F (180°C) for 25-30 minutes. Cool on wire rack and add your favourite icing.

Recipe by Priya dasi

# One Hundred Thousand Bags of Rice

Technology can be great. It makes for a more efficient life. However, as our world becomes more technology-driven, we also crave authentic experiences. If technology supports our relationships, then all is well. If it gets in the way, then our lives can be poorer. There are some experiences so devoid of technology but so rich in relationship that you are left with a sense of wonderment at their existence. Preparing for the once-a-year five-day pilgrimage in West Bengal is such an experience.

Every year, over fifteen thousand people gather to visit special holy places. The spectacle of fifteen thousand people walking, chanting and singing together is extraordinary. Fifteen thousand people for five days also means 225,000 meals. It being India, this means a lot of rice.

As explained elsewhere, my beloved Gurudeva, who started travelling outside India aged seventy-six, spent his last fourteen years perpetually in motion around the globe, speaking of the glories of Radha and Krsna. During his manifest stay in this world, he trained some wonderful younger monks. One of them is known as Tirtha Maharaj.

Tirtha Maharaj is like butter and cream. He is constantly energetic, serving and always soft and loving. In the lead-up to the pilgrimage, he takes a team of devotees and ventures out into the Bengal countryside from village to village, and hut to hut.

For three months, Tirtha Maharaj and his team endure the most austere lifestyle, spreading teachings about loving Krsna, and gaining pledges of rice. One hundred and fifty thousand meals are being collected, rice bag by rice bag.

Somehow, Tirtha Maharaj remembers every pledge, and every bag promised is collected when the time comes and delivered to the temple where the pilgrimage is hosted.

Prasadam is mercy. It is love manifested. From the love of the villagers, the rice is donated. Then the preparations are made with love, offered with devotion, distributed with affection and eaten with a mood of honour and service. Gurudeva said “we don’t eat prasadam, we serve and honour prasadam.”

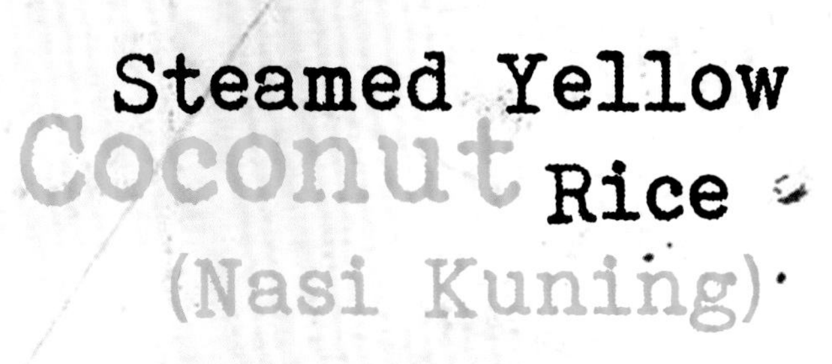

# Steamed Yellow Coconut Rice (Nasi Kuning)

**Serves 4 - preparation and cooking time 20-30 minutes**

**All you need is**

- 2 cups (350 gr) long grain jasmine rice
- 1 cup (240 ml) coconut milk
- 2 cups (480 ml) water
- 1 stem of lemon grass (bottom part crushed)
- 3 kaffir lime leaves*
- 1 tsp (5 ml) of turmeric
- 1 tbsp (15 ml) of salt

**The way**

1. Combine all ingredients in a heavy saucepan. Boil rice on medium heat until all the water is absorbed.
2. Transfer the rice into a steamer. Steam rice for 10-15 minutes.
3. Alternatively you can cook the ingredients in a rice cooker.

* You may substitute the leaves for the juice of 1 lime.

Tip: Serve with Balinese spinach coconut salad, Gado Gado with peanut sauce and or fried tofu in chili sauce and a side of emping.

Recipe by Anupama dasi

All you need is

- Big bunch (approximately 1 lb or 500 gr) fresh spinach
- 2 cups (200 gr) bean sprouts
- 1 cup (250 gr) cucumber cut into small cubes
- 1 cup (80 gr) fresh grated coconut (dried or frozen coconut as an alternative)
- 2 tbsp (30 ml) coconut oil or any other cooking oil
- 1 tbsp (15 ml) fresh ginger, grated
- 1 big red chili seeded and finely chopped
- 1-2 tomatoes cut into wedges
- 1 tsp (5 ml) asafoetida
- 1 tbsp (15 ml) coriander powder
- 1 tsp (5 ml) turmeric powder
- 1 fresh kaffir lime leaf (if available) cut very thin or juice of half a lime
- 1 tsp (5 ml) brown sugar
- 1 1/2 tsp salt (7.5 ml - or to taste)

# Balinese Spinach +Coconut Salad

**Serves 4 - preparation and cooking time 20-25 minutes**

The way

1. Blanch the spinach followed by the sprouts in hot water, do not over cook, then drain and put them aside.
2. Heat oil in a small saucepan on medium heat, add asafoetida, ginger and chili. Stir for a few seconds and add the coriander and turmeric powder. Stir for a few moments.
3. Add the grated coconut, salt, sugar and kaffir lime leaf. Cook it for couple of minutes on slightly lower heat and then add tomatoes.
4. Mix all the veggies and the coconut dressing in a bowl, serve warm or cold.

Tip: You may also start step 2 in a wok (stir-fry pan) and complete the method in it. This recipe is also good with cabbage or beans (string bean or long bean).

Serve with steamed yellow coconut rice, fried tofu in chili and tomato sauce and a side of emping.

Recipe by Anupama dasi

# Two White Elephants

During one of the two pilgrimages each year, a fifteen thousand army of bhakti-yoga practitioners from all over the world treks throughout the countryside. Sometimes, we will wander through a village. Typically, the villagers will stand by the side of the road, smiling and waving. I like singing "Radhe! Radhe!" and they will call back "Radhe! Radhe.". It is very beautiful to connect with foreign people in a foreign land whose language I do not speak. The love of devotional life radiant through their eyes and broad smiles is a feeling I can remember and relish for years.

One year, a dear friend of mine, named Govi, and I decided to get ahead of the crowd. Every so often, the pilgrims would assemble at a temple or a holy place and speakers would tell of ancient pastimes. We skipped ahead and found ourselves in one of the villages. Typically on a pilgrimage, we wake at 4am or 4.30am. Therefore, a late morning snooze can work wonders.

We came across one of these huts. The mother and father were inside their residential space which consisted of a hut and a small covered area. A cow and a calf were tied by a rope to a tree. The parents had three children—an elder boy, a middle sister and a younger boy. Govi made signs to them showing that we were sleepy and needed a lie down. There was a small flurry of activity as the wife obtained two simple straw mats which were laid out side by side. I could not understand anything that was being said, but you could tell from the intonation that they were reaching out to us and wanting to serve us. We were on a pilgrimage and, for them, it was an honour to assist us.

Govi and I lay down to rest in the shady spot that the wife had arranged for us. As I closed my eyes, I felt the family's presence quite intensely. I opened one of my eyes very discreetly, and realised that the whole family was standing over us, watching us like we were exotic aliens. I felt very safe and, while in the West such a scene may have felt odd, it was somehow totally natural. The tallest member of their family was not even a couple of inches over five feet. These two large-bodied westerners must have looked highly unusual to them.

It was a sublime sleep. When we woke we were offered a cup of milk from their cow, which we gratefully accepted. We had benefited from the mercy of the locals who had offered us both hospitality and nourishment. We felt very blessed as we heard the cacophony from our fifteen thousand strong group, which had by this time caught us up and had occupied a nearby field waiting for prasadam to be served.

### All you need is

- 1 lb (500 gr) Tofu
- Oil for frying
- 3 big red chilies, seeded and finely chopped (or more if you like spicy)
- 3-4 medium size tomatoes, cut roughly
- 2 tbsp (30 ml) oil
- 5 candlenuts* cut into small pieces
- 3 Indonesian bay leaves** (optional)
- 3 tbsp (45 ml) palm sugar or brown sugar
- 1 tbsp (15 ml) salt or to taste

* Indonesian bay leaves, called daun salam are available in Asian grocery stores, if not omit them.

** You may substitute candlenuts with macadamia nuts. 1 1/2 macadamia nuts = 1 candlenut.

### The way

1. Cut tofu into 1 inch squares by 1/2 inch in thickness (4x4 cm by 1 cm in thickness).
2. Heat oil in frying pan, shallow fry tofu until golden brown, drain on paper towel and put aside.
3. Blend chilies, tomatoes and candlenuts in a blender until smooth.
4. Heat 2 tbsp oil in frying pan, add the sauce and bay leaves and fry until thick in consistency.
5. Add sugar, salt, fried tofu and stir.
6. Ensure all tofu pieces are covered with sauce and remove from the stove.

**Tip:** Chili can be replaced with red capsicum (bell peppers) if you do not want spicy. This sauce is also good with fried tempeh, fried eggplant or potato.

Serve with steamed yellow coconut rice, Balinese spinach coconut salad and or Gado Gado with peanut sauce and a side of emping.

Recipe by Anupama dasi

# Fried Tofu
## in Chili
## & Tomato Sauce

Serves 4 - preparation and cooking time 20-25 minutes

# Gado Gado
## Indonesian Steamed Veggie Salad

**Serves 4 - preparation and cooking time 30 minutes**

All you need for Gado Gado

- 1 1/2 cups of each of the following: cabbage, string beans, potato, bean sprouts and cucumber cut into bite size pieces.
- 7 oz (200 gr) tempeh
- 7 oz (200 gr) tofu
- Oil for deep-frying tempeh and tofu
- Salt to taste

Peanut Sauce Ingredients

- 1 1/2 cups (250 gr) raw peanuts*
- 1 big red chili or 1-2 green chili seeded, finely chopped
- 1/2 cup (120 ml) coconut milk
- 1/2-1 cup (120-240 ml) water
- 2-4 kaffir lime leaves, slightly torn and crushed (or juice of a lime)
- 1/2 lemon juiced
- 1/4 cup (50 gr) palm sugar (or brown sugar)
- 2 tbsp (30 ml) cooking oil
- 3 tbsp (45 ml) Indonesian sweet soy sauce (kecap manis)
- 2 tsp (10 ml) salt (or to taste)

* You may substitute peanuts with 3/4 cup (150 gr) peanut butter. You will then omit frying and food processing. Instead add the peanut butter to the oil and chili with the rest of the ingredients.

Tip: Serve with steamed yellow coconut rice, fried tofu in chili tomato sauce and a side of emping.

Recipe by Anupama dasi

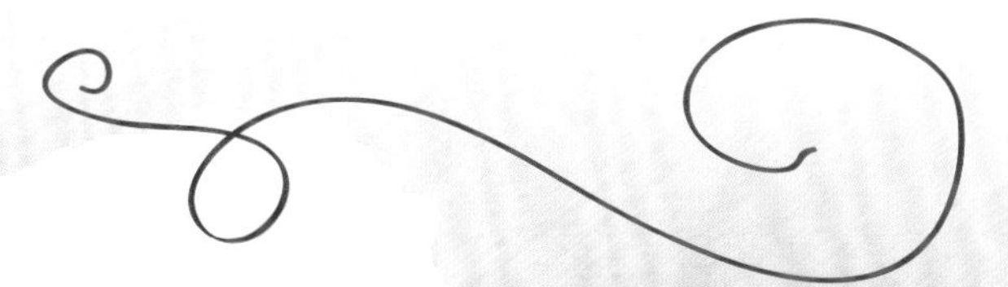

The way

1. Cube and boil potatoes, cut veggies in small pieces, steam all except the sprouts and cucumber and put aside.

2. Cut tempe and tofu into 1/2 inch (1.25 cm) cubes and deep-fry until golden brown and a little crispy. Drain on paper towel, lightly salt and put aside.

3. Make peanut sauce. Heat the oil, add chili and peanuts and fry for 2 minutes.

4. Grind the peanuts, chili and 1/2 of the water until smooth in a blender or food processor.

5. Put the peanut mixture and the rest of the peanut sauce ingredients in saucepan over low heat, add more water to thin out the sauce and stir with a wooden spoon.

6. Watch over it as it will boil and bubble. After cooking for a few minutes, take it off the heat and drizzle generously over veggies, fried tempeh and tofu.

# No-One Eats Alone

Love is a verb. We feel it. It causes us to act, to serve and to please the object of our love. Pleasing our lover or loved one fills us with love. It makes us happy. When I love someone I am happy to please that person even if that person does not know that I was the one making the arrangement.

When I met Srila Gurudeva, he was seventy-six years old. He had never left India; but, until his departure from the vision of this world, embarked on thirty-one world tours in fourteen years until 2010. I remember when, aged eighty-eight, he was scheduled to undertake a tour that would have challenged a thirty-year-old man. Srila Gurudeva's utter devotion to Radha-Krishna inspired him to perform extraordinary activities. He had heard that hundreds of followers were waiting at a festival celebrating bhakti-yoga in Italy. So strong and deep was his affection, so active was this principle of love, that he eschewed any rest and flew from the USA to Italy within twenty-four hours of the end of his American tour. He wanted us all to experience this love. This is why he would encourage us to go on two pilgrimages every year to holy places in India, one in Vrindavana about three hours from Delhi, and one in Navadwip, about three hours from Calcutta.

The Navadwip pilgrimage attracted in excess

Fifteen thousand people are glorifying prasadam:

# Maha-Prasadam ki Jaya!"

of fifteen thousand people. It is an extraordinary spectacle. Everyday, three times a day, prasadam is prepared for everyone. The organiser of this prasadam is a wonderful monk named Premananda Prabhu. Prema is the highest love in the universe, and ananda means bliss. This name nicely describes how he prepares the prasadam for thousands every day. Under him there are young men and women helping, buying, cutting, stirring, preparing and serving. Some of the pots are larger than Jacuzzis. When it is time to serve prasadam, we all gather in lines, shoulder to shoulder, with one leaf plate each, waiting for one of the men to serve us one preparation after another. Someone will cry out "Maha-Prasadam ki" and all who have assembled will cry back "jai" which mean "victory or glories". So, "All glories to Krishna prasadam" Fifteen thousand people are glorifying prasadam. This is the same as glorifying the mercy of Radha-Krishna who are trying to make our spiritual evolution easier, as Their mercy melts our hearts through prasadam.

No-one eats alone. We are one family. We are brothers and sisters whether we are white, brown, black or yellow. We all share the same goal, which is to be recipients of mercy and to soften our hearts so that we may feel how truly Krishna loves us and how deeply we can love Him.

# Making The Offering

Gurudeva emphasised function over form when offering our food. He taught me how the number-one ingredient in any offering is affection, and sincerity. This is what Radha-Krishna relish.

Handed down through the millennia from the transcendental masters of an ancient era to Gurudeva's guru's guru to Gurudeva, we have some powerful meditations for when we offer food.

I start out by saying, or thinking, "I am happily preparing myself for making this offering of love by meditating on Gurudeva, who is Radha-Krishna's associate. He is personally connecting me with Them." It may seem like God is far away. It can feel like Radha-Krishna are abstract. But this is one of the magnificent functions of Gurudeva, even if he appears to be no longer on the planet. If I do not have the eyes to see Radha-Krishna, Gurudeva can give me vision. We have the opportunity to let him be our transparent via-medium.

It is always a simple process. Even though it is the Supreme Lord of worlds and all beings who we are welcoming in to eat our offering, the mood is one of intimacy, sweetness and affection. After welcoming Gurudeva, I welcome Them and offer Them, in my mind, a beautiful seat. Often I will offer real flowers to Them. If flowers are not available, I do this in my mind.

"Please accept this offering of love," I pray. I then chant the names of Radha-Krishna:

*Hare Krishna Hare Krishna*
*Krishna Krishna Hare Hare*
*Hare Rama Hare Rama*
*Rama Rama Hare Hare*

Keep a separate plate, and cup (for water), for Radha-Krishna. Once your food preparation has been completed, you can serve it using Their plate and cup. Just place Their plate and cup in front of Their picture (see next page). After a few minutes, you then transfer whatever was on Their plate back into the preparation pots. Now it is all prasadam! And you can serve this with joy to your family, guests or whomever you are serving prasadam to.

I always remember that this is about love and affection. Stick with this simple process and have love in your heart, and you and those around you will benefit enormously.

If you want to develop your offering rituals further with more intricacies and the original Sanskrit mantras, then please visit

**www.kitchenoflove.com**

# The Altar

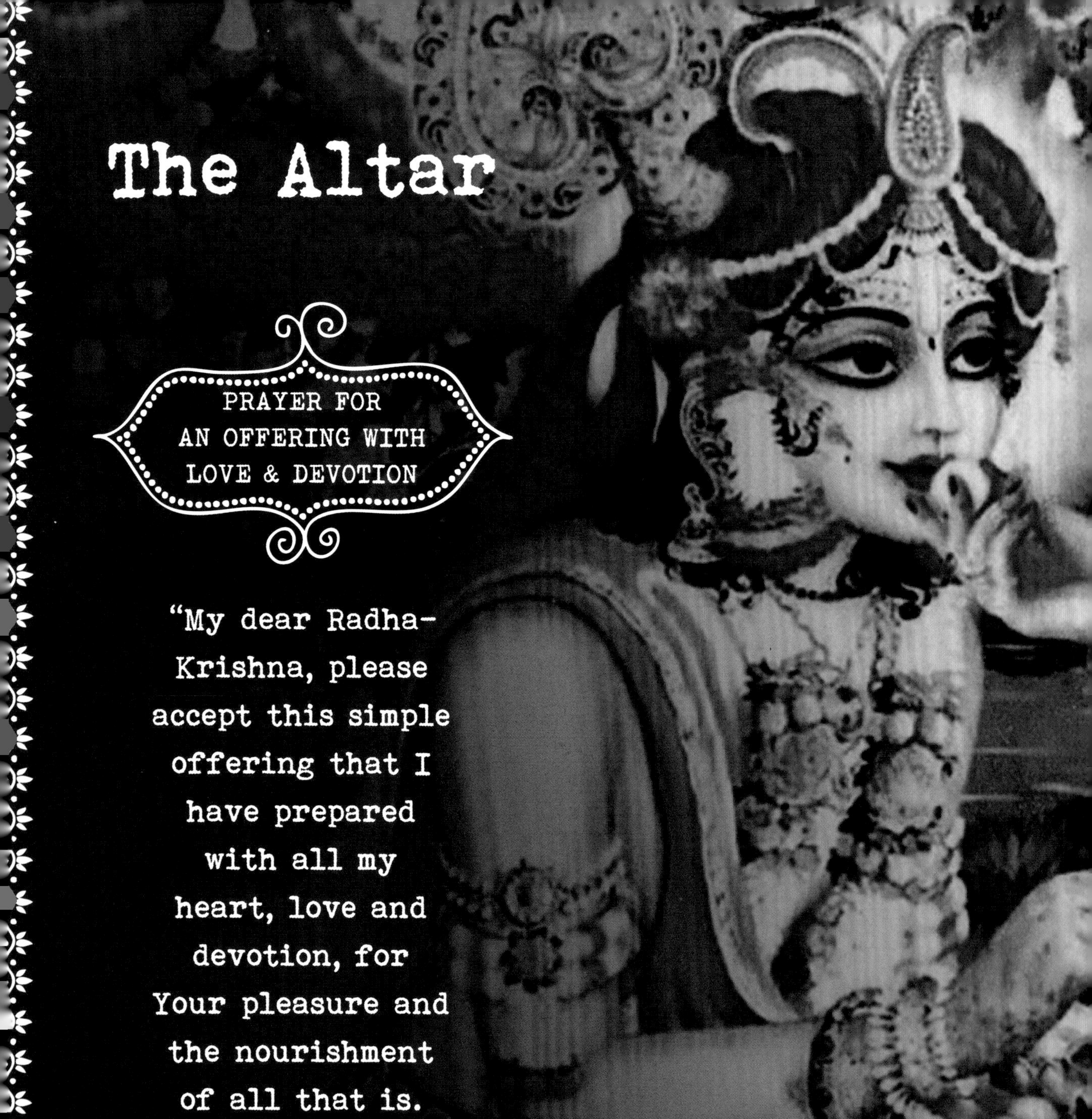

PRAYER FOR
AN OFFERING WITH
LOVE & DEVOTION

"My dear Radha-Krishna, please accept this simple offering that I have prepared with all my heart, love and devotion, for Your pleasure and the nourishment of all that is. Hare Krishna!"

sattva-guna
[pure goodness] ...

# TIMELESS WISDOM FROM THE *Bhagavad-gita*

Foods that bequeath longevity, full of energy, bestow good health and vigour with happiness and satisfaction are relished by those in sattva-guna the mode of goodness. Such foods in sattva-guna particularly increase life and are juicy, savoury, rich and nourishing, like invigorating serum, which remains long in the body, and are agreeable and pleasing to the palate. Foods of this type which are chewed, licked, sucked and drunk are relished by those situated in sattva-guna.

# Fried Tofu Dumplings

## in Sweet & Sour Sauce

Serves 4-6 - preparation and cooking time 35-45 minutes

### All you need for Dumplings

- 14 oz (400 gr) firm tofu, cubed into 2 cm pieces
- Tofu Seasoning:
- 3 tbsp (15 ml) soy sauce, 3 tbsp tomato ketchup (15 ml) and pepper to taste
- Tofu batter:
- 1/2 cup (120 gr) of self-raising flour
- 1/4 cup (40 gr) corn flour (cornstarch)
- 3 tbsp (45 gr) rice flour
- 1/2–3/4 cup (120–180 ml) water
- 1 tsp (5 ml) salt
- Black pepper (to taste)
- Cooking oil to deep-fry dumplings

### Method for Dumplings

1. Marinate tofu pieces in seasoning while making sauce.
2. Combine remaining ingredients to form a smooth batter, slightly thicker than pancake batter.
3. Drain the tofu pieces.
4. Coat individual tofu pieces then deep fry until golden brown and crunchy.
5. Drain on a paper towel and set aside.

**Note:** Dumplings go soggy when left in sauce for too long.

offered by Anupama dasi

### All you need for Sauce

- 1/2 cup diced bell pepper (1 red or yellow bell pepper)
- 1/2 cup sliced celery
- 1/2 cup frozen green peas
- 1/2 cup pineapple chunks
- 1/2 cup snap peas
- 1 tbsp (15 ml) grated ginger
- 1/2 a red chili seeded and thinly sliced
- 2 tbsp (30 ml) cooking oil
- 1/2 tsp (2.5 ml) sesame oil
- 1 tbsp (15 ml) corn flour (mixed with 5 tbsp water)
- 1 1/2 cups (360 ml) water
- 3 tbsp (45 ml) soy sauce
- a little less than 1/2 cup (100 ml) tomato ketchup
- a little less than 1/2 cup (100 ml) tomato puree
- 3 tbsp brown sugar
- Salt and black pepper (to taste)

### Method for Sauce

1. Heat both oils in a medium saucepan.
2. Add ginger and chili.
3. Fry for ten seconds then add the tomato sauce, soy sauce and water.
4. Add all vegetables and simmer for three minutes then turn down the flame.
5. Add the cornstarch, mix well.
6. Once thickened add brown sugar, salt, black pepper then turn off heat.
7. Arrange tofu dumplings on plate and pour sauce over the top. Serve immediately and with rice.

# Tempeh Sauerkraut Cheese Melt

## open sandwich

**Serves 4 - preparation and cooking time 20-25 minutes**

### Ingredients

- 14 oz (400 gr) tempeh
- 4 tbsp (60 ml) olive oil
- 1/4 tsp (1.25 ml) sesame oil
- 1 tsp (5 ml) asafoetida
- 1 tbsp (15 ml) soy sauce
- 10.5 oz (300 gr) sauerkraut
- 1 tbsp (15 ml) butter
- 1 tsp (5 ml) butter
- Salt to taste
- 8 thick slices of vegetarian Swiss cheese
- 8 rustic bread slices
- Mustard
- Tomato slices

### Method

1. Slice tempeh in thin rectangular pieces (to fit the size of the rustic bread).
2. Heat the oils in the pan on medium heat. Add tempeh and fry on both sides until crispy (you may need to add more oil).
3. Add 1 tbsp butter and asafoetida, then drizzle soy sauce over tempeh.
4. Heat sauerkraut in a pan with 1 tsp butter with a drizzle of soy sauce.
5. Spread mustard generously on bread followed by a layer of sauerkraut, tomatoes, tempeh and cheese.
6. Put under a broiler (or grill) for a few minutes while the cheese melts.

**Tip:** Serve with a salad and chips. Try with lettuce and alfalfa sprouts on top.

Recipe by BV Vaikhanas Maharaja

# Lemon Cake with Lemon Mascarpone Icing

Serves 6-8 - preparation and cooking time 1 hour and 10 minutes

**All you need for cake**

- 1/2 cup (120 gr) butter, softened
- 2 tsp (10 ml) finely grated lemon rind
- 1 1/4 cups (225 gr) caster sugar (finely granulated)
- 3 tbsp of sour cream (or other egg replacer)
- 1 1/2 cups (200 gr) self-raising flour
- 1 tsp (5 ml) baking soda (bicarbonate of soda)
- 1/2 cup (120 ml) milk
- 1/4 cup (60 ml) lemon juice

**For icing**

- 9 oz (250 gr) mascarpone cheese
- 7 oz (200 gr) grams whipping cream
- 1 cup (115 gr) powdered sugar (icing sugar)
- 2 tsp (10 ml) finely grated lemon rind
- Chopped macadamia nuts for sprinkling (optional)

**The way**

1. Preheat oven to 350°F (180°C) (or 325°F /160°C fan-forced). Grease a deep cake tin, 8 inch (20 cm) in diameter and line base with baking paper.

2. Make icing. Beat the cream, sifted icing sugar and lemon rind in a small bowl with an electric mixer until soft peaks form. Fold mascarpone into mixture. Cover and refrigerate until required.

3. Make cake batter. Beat butter, lemon rind and sugar in small bowl with electric mixer until light and fluffy. Add sour cream (or other egg replacer) and mix till just combined. Transfer to large bowl. Stir in sifted flour, milk and juice.

4. Pour mixture into tin and bake about 50 minutes (ovens may vary). Stand cake 5 minutes. Cool on wire rack.

5. Split cake into 2 layers and spread lemon mascarpone icing in between layers (optional) or simply spread icing all over the top and sides of cake without splitting the cake.

6. Sprinkle macadamia nuts on top of cake.

offered by Damayanti dasi

"Love has nothing to take, yet every-thing to give..."
– Swami BV Narayana

# Conclusion

You can utilise your offering to transport yourself to the magical realm of the Divine Couple in the spiritual world.

When I first travelled to India in 1996, I felt transformed by the immediacy and intensity of spiritual emotion that I perceived pulsating in the hearts of the people I met. And this included everyday people. Everybody was radiating a certain something that I had never experienced before.

While the masters of bhakti-yoga have been great intellectuals, some speaking nine languages, this path recognises that ultimately the intimate association with Radha-Krishna depends on the ecstasy of spiritual emotion pouring through the heart. The serving of prasadam and the development of this connection has helped me in this way.

I have been taught to visualise Radha and Krishna in the spiritual world, residing in the realm of Goloka Vrindavana. They spend Their time in the beautiful groves of Braj, in the kunds (lakes) throughout Vrindavana and Braj, and in the forests and groves. Gurudeva is there. He is serving Radha-Krishna.

So I offer my food to Gurudeva and ask that he will, in turn, offer it to Radha-Krishna. Radha and Krishna relish the offering, imbuing it with Their own love and affection. Gurudeva then distributes Their prasadam to all the inhabitants in the spiritual world.

Now, supercharged with the devotion of the Divine Couple, Their friends and Gurudeva, the prasadam is passed by Gurudeva back to me. This way my tongue, instead of chasing the next thing to enjoy and then forget, ingests this divine love and transports me closer and closer to the spiritual world. Over time, I increasingly realize the reality of this connection in the heart. The goal of bhakti is for our spiritual nature to prevail. When this occurs, our attraction to temporary things will naturally dwindle. One day we will, by the mercy of Gurudeva, reside in the association of the Divine Couple – and while in this world function with Their power.

## BHAKTI ON THE WEB

*Get in touch with us!*

**Your path to bhakti begins here.**

Visit one of our websites to learn more:

www.purebhakti.com • www.backtobhakti.com
www.purebhakti.tv • www.harikatha.com
www.bhaktistore.com • www.bhaktigifts.com
www.gvpbookdistribution.com

Join us on www.kitchenoflove.com